BASIC TO C
C

BOOK TO BE RETURNED ON OR
BEFORE DATE STAMPED BELOW

BASIC TO C
CONVERSION MANUAL

23023 5.

ROBERT J. TRAISTER

PRENTICE-HALL, INC., Englewood Cliffs, New Jersey 07632

Library of Congress Cataloging-in-Publication Data

Traister, Robert J.
  BASIC to C conversion manual.

  Includes index.
  1. BASIC (Computer program language)
  2. C (Computer program language)   I. Title.
  II. Title: Basic to C conversion.
  QA76.73.B3T75   1987   005.13′3   86-30490
  ISBN 0-13-058363-4

Editorial/production supervision and
   interior design: Nancy Menges/David Ershun
Cover design: Whitman Studio, Inc.
Manufacturing buyer: S. Gordon Osbourne

Printed in the United States of America

10 9 8 7 6 5 4 3 2

ISBN   0-13-058363-4   025

PRENTICE-HALL INTERNATIONAL (UK) LIMITED, *London*
PRENTICE-HALL OF AUSTRALIA PTY. LIMITED, *Sydney*
PRENTICE-HALL CANADA INC., *Toronto*
PRENTICE-HALL HISPANOAMERICANA, S.A., *Mexico*
PRENTICE-HALL OF INDIA PRIVATE LIMITED, *New Delhi*
PRENTICE-HALL OF JAPAN, INC., *Tokyo*
PRENTICE-HALL OF SOUTHEAST ASIA PTE. LTD., *Singapore*
EDITORA PRENTICE-HALL DO BRASIL, LTDA., *Rio de Janeiro*

This book is dedicated to my good friends, Ed and Peggy Shokes

Contents

Preface

Today, C is the language used by most major software developers for writing all of their applications. C is portable, fast, efficient, and offers a structure that is easy to read and comprehend. C has been called a shorthand version of assembly language. Therefore, programmers who regularly use assembly language can adapt rapidly to the syntax of C. However, programmers who use other languages will probably have much more difficulty learning C. This is especially true of BASIC programmers, who tend to experience the most difficulty.

This manual is designed to help you over many of these difficulties. When you are learning a foreign language, a translation guide or foreign language dictionary is most helpful. This, then, is the "foreign language" dictionary for C, written to be understandable by BASIC programmers.

All of the most-used Microsoft BASIC statements and functions are listed, along with their C language counterparts. Some BASIC statements are converted to special C functions; others are evoked through in-program constructs.

This manual is the result of listening to students' questions throughout the many BASIC to C seminars I have taught. I hope that the most-asked questions are answered in the following pages.

Your journey from BASIC to C is an important one, but it need not be filled with frustration. With this manual and any good, full-featured C programming environment, learning C will be a most rewarding experience—one that you will look back on with pleasure.

I would like to thank Lifeboat Associates, Tarrytown, New York, for supplying the Lattice C compiler used for researching this book.

Robert J. Traister

CHAPTER ONE

Introduction

Learning is always a matter of converting—converting known quantities and experiences into equivalencies in the new or unknown field. Therefore, when BASIC language programmers begin learning C language, they will automatically begin to make conversions mentally. The conversions are most clearly explained by the ratio method, or "This is to BASIC as that is to C." Through such conversions, comprehension can come more quickly, provided that the comparisons being made are accurate ones.

If you are trying to learn C language with only a BASIC background, you are certainly finding that the transition is not a simple matter of making conversions. The differences in the two languages make immediate comparisons difficult. Fortunately, after a bit more knowledge is gained, making the necessary comparisons comes more easily.

BASIC and C share many, many traits. This is not obvious at first glance because of the syntax of C. Nevertheless, it is true. While writing CBREEZE, the BASIC to C tutorial translator software package, I gained an intimate understanding of the relationships between these two languages. Indeed, it was necessary to duplicate many BASIC functions and statements through C language functions. BASIC functions such as MID$, RIGHT$, LEFT$, and the like, had no direct counterparts that were part of the C language's standard function set. When these BASIC functions were encountered by the translator, they were translated as special C functions I had written previously to mimic their operations. The same is true of CLS, LOCATE, CSRLIN, POS, and the like, in BASIC. These statements accomplish machine-dependent operations and are not a part of the standard C language function set. Again, special C functions were built from the standard function set to mimic these operations.

The authors of C wisely kept the language small by providing a limited number of functions. From this small function set, many special or personalized functions could be built that would address the more elaborate and machine-dependent computer operations.

This text goes a step further and shows how many of the Microsoft BASIC statements and functions may be produced in C language through specialized C functions or through standard C constructs. The functions may be thought of as miniature programs or subroutines. Indeed, all of them may be incorporated in any C program or may be called from another C program if they are left in their function formats. It is hoped that by studying these small portions of C code and the comments that accompany them, a better understanding of C language will be gained within the Framework of BASIC, the language you currently know best.

A special section of this book is devoted to duplicating BASIC math functions in C. Today, most C compilers are equipped with the UNIX math functions such as sqrt(), pow(), sin(), cos(), and so forth; but this was not true only a few years ago. However, the quality of these math functions may vary from good to very poor, depending on the compiler or C programming environment being used. Also, many readers may have inherited one of the older compilers that is devoid of any of the higher math functions. The source code for these functions will be mandatory in the latter instance. However, the source code for the math functions provided in these pages is very versatile and can be used to improve the math-handling capabilities of even the most modern compiler.

Still other sections deal with string-handling functions and with strings in C in general. This is an area that many beginners seem to have problems with. What is a string in C? What is a character string pointer? How is it different from an array of characters? All of these questions and more are answered in these pages.

The concept of *pointers* is quite foreign to BASIC programmers, but these special variables are a mainstay for C programmers. One chapter of this manual deals solely with the subject of pointers. How do you initialize a pointer? How do you change a variable into a pointer? When should pointers be used? When should they not be used? How do pointers allow ''peek and poke'' operations? All of these questions are answered.

The primary purpose of this manual is to help the beginning C programmer who has only a BASIC background learn to program in C. However, its purpose does not end there. As your experience grows, this book will grow with you, taking you further into this language than you could ever do on your own. Whether your question lies in the area of general syntax, function construction, pointers, strings, or even the most complex math functions, this text is a guide that will go with you every step of the way.

SIMPLE CONVERSION

To illustrate the direction this text will take, the following C function will mimic the actions of BASIC's INPUT statement when it is used to display a prompt and to retrieve a string argument from the keyboard:

```
/* p = prompt phrase; s = input variable */
input(p, s)
char *p, *s;
{

        printf("%s ", p);   /* Display prompt */
        gets(s);        /* Get keyboard input */

}
```

This function might be called from a C program in the following manner:

```
main()
{

        char a[40], b[40];

        strcpy(a, "Input your name");

        input(a, b);
        puts(b);

}
/* Source code for input() goes here */
```

The calling program assigns char array a[] the value of the prompt, while the b[] array is made large enough to hold a 39-character input from the keyboard. When the special function named input() is called, it uses arrays a[] and b[] as arguments. Within the function, the value of a[] is displayed on the screen using printf(). The gets() function is used to read keyboard input, assigning the retrieved characters to b[]. This use of C code allows us to construct the special C function, input(), which duplicates some of the operation of INPUT in BASIC.

Now, INPUT is a very complex BASIC statement that may be used in many different ways. It can be used with or without a prompt argument. It may be used to retrieve any type of keyboard input—integer, float, or string. It may be used to assign more than one variable. The list goes on. It is certainly feasible to write a C function that will do all of these things as well, but from a tutorial standpoint, it would be too complex to be useful in teaching C language to a novice audience. Most of the examples in this book will be made as simple as possible to gain the best tutorial advantage. Therefore, some statements and functions in BASIC will be only partially supported by their C function counterparts in this text.

Throughout this book, BASIC functions and statements will be mimicked or duplicated by C functions, where desirable, or by means of simple C language constructs. Through examination of these functions and constructs, the C language student who knows BASIC should derive a better understanding of the new language.

WHY A BASIC TO C CONVERSION MANUAL?

This manual has come about because of events that took place in my life in 1982. At that time, I was a fairly accomplished BASIC language programmer who wrote books about computer programs for a living. In the early 1980s, C was a language that was virtually unknown to most microcomputer programmers who did not make a living programming. I had written several programming books for one of my publishers, and one day, I received a call that was to lead me in a completely different direction. This publisher asked if I would research and write a book on C language.

At first I was hesitant, as I knew absolutely nothing about C language. However, a very lucrative contract and a very ample project completion time soon convinced me to take the assignment. Little did I suspect the headaches this acceptance would cause me, not only in the ensuing months but for several years to come.

I scanned every computer magazine I had on hand for a C language programming environment. I finally found one in the form of a compiler from a fairly well known company. Remember, back in the early 1980s, C was almost unknown to microcomputer hobbyists. Those were the days when almost every microcomputer owner programmed in BASIC Interpreter and nothing else. At this point, I had never used a compiler and really didn't understand what that type of environment did.

To make a long story even longer, I persuaded the compiler company to send me their latest C compiler at no charge to be used as the model compiler for the book. I expected to receive something akin to the Microsoft BASIC Interpreter package, except that it would be a compiler for C. I anticipated that the package would include a very complete manual that would also serve as a tutorial. I figured that my ''in-depth'' BASIC language knowledge (by my standards) would more than prepare me to tackle this new language. I have never been more wrong in my life!

The only C language book in print at this time (to my knowledge) was *The C Programming Language*, by Kernighan and Ritchie (known as K&R). This is an excellent reference source, but by the authors' own admission, it is definitely *not* a tutorial. To make matters even worse, the documentation that accompanied the C compiler I received can only be described as horrible.

After 30 days of trying, I had yet to successfully compile and run my first program. I worked for hours on end, trying everything imaginable, and still ended up with nothing. Repeated calls to the compiler supplier brought helpful suggestions. They instructed me how to write a program (using EDLIN in MS-DOS). Their documentation assumed that the user already knew how to use a compiler. I did not.

At the end of this 30-day period, I was pulling my hair out and regretting the day I ever got involved with C. I called the compiler company again and spoke to people in the technical assistance department, who by this time knew me on a first name basis (the first name being ''Dummy''). I was told that they had recently done some testing on the compiler version I was sent and had found that it didn't work! I was then asked if I would like them to send me a working version. (This has to have been the most ridiculous question I have ever been asked.) When the new compiler arrived (with the same *bad* documentation), I excitedly tried out K&R's famous starter program:

```
main()
{

    printf("hello, world\n");

}
```

To my dismay, the program would compile, but the assembly language output would not pass through IBM's Macro Assembler. Again, I spent weeks trying to get my first working program. Out of desperation, I again called the compiler company. This time, I talked with a new technician. After hearing my problems, he deduced that I had a bad compiler. Again I was sent a new model. This time, it worked! After 45 days, I had finally compiled K&R's ''hello, world'' program!

From this point on, things were not milk and honey by any stretch of the imagination. The working model of this compiler was very limited. It did not follow the Kernighan and Ritchie standard—offered no floating point operations—and worst of all, many of the standard functions it did support simply would not work. Over a year later, I read a review of this compiler in a popular computer magazine. The reviewer's main complaints were that the documentation was absolutely useless and that many of the functions simply did not work.

I struggled along with these handicaps and finally did complete a very primitive book on learning C language. By today's standards, the book would be classified as trite; but back then, many BASIC programmers were having the same problems in learning C that I was. My mistakes and misfortunes and, more important, what I had learned from them were appreciated by a large number of readers who purchased this book.

When my first book on C was finished, I was bound and determined never to delve into this area again. Several months later, I received a complimentary copy of the Lattice C compiler in response to some correspondence I had sent out when writing the infamous C book. I looked at the software in disgust and promptly threw it in a little-used desk drawer with the intention of possibly sending it to any enemies I might make in the computer programming world in the future.

Several months later, I had completed a writing assignment and didn't feel like starting another book for a while. My boredom led me to that same little-used desk drawer. I pulled out the Lattice C compiler and decided to "play" with it a bit.

Miracle of miracles! *This* compiler was easy to use, and its documentation was simple and accurate. Most miraculous of all, this compiler would quickly compile all of the examples K&R had included in their reference book! Whereas the first compiler I had used would take at least five minutes to compile even the simplest program, the Lattice C compiler took only a minute or so. This compiler was easy, almost pleasant to use.

It was from this accidental reacquaintance with C that I began to delve deeply into the subject. However, learning C was still not an easy task. It would take years. The reason for this was the relatively unknown nature of C in a microcomputer environment. But this was changing. Eventually, C began making inroads into the microcomputer field, and study manuals began popping up from a few publishers. These manuals were aimed at the BASIC programmer who wanted to learn C. I wrote several more texts on the subject and am still doing so today.

The big handicap to BASIC programmers who want to learn C is the fact that BASIC in no way prepares the programmer to begin to grasp the basics of C. However, once these basics have been learned, students who know BASIC can progress more rapidly, because they can begin to see strong relationships between the two languages.

THEN CAME CBREEZE

Late in 1983, I was trying to develop a new concept in teaching C. More accurately, I was trying to improve on an old concept. The books that were on the market to teach BASIC programmers C language all used simple BASIC programs as examples. These would then be translated into C. However, if the author did not choose examples that were known to or used by the reader, much of the lesson was lost. I had thought of writing a C tutorial that would include a free consultation coupon to send to me, the author. Then I could answer the readers' specific questions. However, it soon became apparent that if the book was even a mild success, I would be deluged with queries and would not be able to answer them all without working on that and that alone for many months.

It occurred to me that if someone could write a program that would translate BASIC program into C language, it would be the ideal teaching aid. I sat down at my computer and immediately began mapping out such a program.

Three months later, I had developed an extraordinarily crude BASIC to C translator that was written in BASIC. I did this because C compilers were available only for a handful of machines, whereas BASIC could be run on all of them.

However, this first translator—called CGEN, for C generator—would have required a 300-page manual just to describe the restrictions it placed on input code. Its scope was very limited, and any user would outgrow it in a short period of time. It supported only the most elementary BASIC programs and constructs.

I gave up on the idea of a BASIC to C translator and began to write other tutorials on the subject. I noticed that one or two companies were advertising BASIC to C translators about a year later, and I assumed that someone had capitalized on my original idea. However, I arranged to examine each of these translators and found that they could not be used to teach C programming. Although they did translate many BASIC programs into C, the C code was very nonstandard and depended on a large number of special, hidden functions to arrive at a compilable program. They were designed specifically to allow BASIC programs to run faster under C.

In early 1985, I again took a look at the original CGEN program. It was obvious that a truly useful BASIC to C translator that would serve as the best available C training aid could not be written in BASIC, at least not from a practical standpoint. So I threw out CGEN altogether and began again from scratch. This time, the translator was written in Lattice C. During the time I had given up on CGEN and started this latest translator, C compilers had become available for most types of microcomputers, so portability was no longer a problem.

It was not possible to salvage anything from CGEN, other than the inherent understanding that writing the program had provided me in knowing where direct conversions from BASIC to C could be made and where other types of conversions were necessary. If nothing else, CGEN had demonstrated that there is a definite and direct relationship between BASIC and C—one that can be used to good tutorial advantage.

Approximately one year later, CBREEZE was completed. This BASIC to C tutorial translator is everything CGEN was not. Users are not greatly restricted in the types of BASIC programs that can be translated into C language. The output C code adheres strictly to the Kernighan and Ritchie standard. It even follows the format standard regarding whitespacing, indentation, and general program appearance.

Since its introduction, CBREEZE has taught thousands of BASIC programmers to program in C.

This reference manual is an offshoot of the CBREEZE project. It draws on my experiences in writing CBREEZE and in establishing direct conversions of BASIC statements, functions, and constructs to pure C language. It is hoped that this manual will speed you on your way to becoming proficient in C language in the shortest time possible.

The reason for this manual, for CBREEZE, and for other tutorial texts I have written is to make it far easier for today's BASIC programmer to learn C. The horror story I related earlier was shared by many others who made the transition from BASIC to C during the early part of this decade. Today, learning C is easier because the language is not so obscure, there are many texts on the subject, and the market abounds with many good C programming environments. With the coming of software tutorials and tutorial translators like CBREEZE, the study of C language will be tackled by more and more BASIC programmers. C has been called the best language for microcomputers. Whether this is true or not remains to be seen, but without a doubt, if you are determined to learn C today, the materials and environments are available. The only thing that can slow you up in this endeavor is frustration. It is hoped that this manual will decrease that factor to a bare minimum.

CHAPTER TWO

Writing Your Own Functions

The C language is small compared to most other languages. It consists of very few statements, but it does have an adequate assortment of functions. These functions have been created from the built-in statements and mathematical operations to form a set of tools from which more elaborate operations can be constructed.

One of the most advantageous features of C (especially when compared to BASIC) is that it allows the programmer to build specialized functions that are not addressed by the standard set of functions. In this chapter, you will learn how to write your own functions, which can then be called from any C language program. One must remember that the standard functions, such as printf, strcpy, strlen, and so forth, were built using C language primitives. The standard function set encompasses the minimum tool set this language's developers felt necessary. As a programmer, you will find it necessary to build still other functions using this basic set.

A C language function is sometimes compared with a subroutine in BASIC. Such subroutines are accessed using the BASIC statement GOSUB. However, this comparison is a poor one. In C, a function is indeed a type of subroutine, but it is one that is separate from the calling program. This means that standard variables used within the calling program are completely unknown to the function unless they are specifically passed as a function argument. Likewise, the variables that are used internally by the function are completely separate and unknown to the calling program unless their values are specifically passed back to the calling program. Admittedly, this seems confusing at first, but a few examples should clear up any confusion.

The following BASIC program uses a subroutine to implement a time delay loop:

```
10   PRINT "HELLO"
20   GOSUB 70
30   PRINT "GOODBYE"
40   GOSUB 70
50   PRINT "ENDING PROGRAM"
60   END
70   FOR X%=0 TO 1000
80   NEXT X%
90   RETURN
```

After each PRINT statement line, the subroutine is entered that causes a delay in executing the next PRINT statement line while the FOR-NEXT loop within the subroutine counts from 0 to 1000.

We can do the same thing in C with the following program:

```
main()
{

        printf("HELLO\n");
        dlay();
        printf("GOODBYE\n");
        dlay();
        printf("ENDING PROGRAM\n");

}
dlay()
{

        int x;

        for (x == 0; x <= 1000; ++x)
               ;

}
```

In this example, a C language function has been created and named dlay. You will notice that the function resides *outside* the body of the calling program, which is the program portion headed by main(). Within the body of the function, an integer variable is declared, and this variable is counted from 0 to 1000 within a for loop. All that is necessary to call the function is to use its name. Within the calling program, you will see dlay(); used twice. Each time this function is encountered within the calling program, it is executed. The function figuratively takes control, and the calling program is not in control until the function has finished executing. After a return from a function call, the next line within the calling program is executed.

This also occurs after a return from a BASIC GOSUB, but there are distinct differences. In the BASIC program example, the value of X% is known outside the subroutine. At any time within this program, the value of X% could have displayed on the screen (using PRINT). At no time in the C program is the value of x known by the calling program. It is usually best to think of a C function as a completely separate program that is called by another program. Although comparisons are made between BASIC GOSUB and C functions, a better comparison can be made between the BASIC CHAIN statement and the program chained to and C functions.

Now let's try another example, first in BASIC and then in C. The BASIC program looks like this:

```
10    INPUT X%
20    GOSUB 50
30    PRINT X%
40    END
50    X%=X%*2
60    RETURN
```

Would the C equivalent look like this?

```
main()
{

      int x;

      scanf("%d", &x);                    WRONG!!
      x = mult(x);
      printf("%d\n", x);

}
mult()
{

      x = x * 2;

}
```

The C language example is utterly and completely wrong, but it does illustrate the type of error many beginning C programmers make when dealing with personally written functions. Here, a function has been named mult(), and its purpose is to multiply the value of x times two, just as the subroutine in the BASIC example did. However, this C program will not return the value of x multiplied by two. As a matter of fact, it won't even compile or run at all on the interpreter, because x will show up as an undeclared variable.

Variable x in the calling program is a different variable altogether from the one found in the function. The function has no way of knowing what the value of x within the calling program is.

For the function to know the value of one or more variables within the calling program, the value or variable must be passed to the function. This is called an *argument to the function.*

The following C program is another wrong attempt at duplicating the BASIC example presented earlier, but it is closer to a working program than the previous C example:

```
main()
{

        int x;

        scanf("%d", &x);
        x = mult(x);                          WRONG!!
        printf("%d\n", x);

}
mult(c)
int c;
{

        c = c * 2;

}
```

In this example, mult() is called with an argument (x). This variable represents the value retrieved from the keyboard by scanf. The value is passed to the function named mult. Notice that mult is defined by name at the bottom of the program and that a variable is inserted within the declaration line. The variable used in the mult declaration is arbitrarily named c. It could just as well have been any other variable name, including x. If it was x, however, this would be a completely different variable from the one named x in the calling program. Either way, the variable named in the function declaration line will be equal to the value of the argument that was passed when mult was called from the main program.

Within the function, c is declared an int. It is absolutely essential that arguments passed to functions be properly declared within the function body. Now variable c in the function is equal to the *value* of variable x in the calling program, since the value of x was passed by the calling program to the function.

However, this program still will not work properly, although it will compile or run without an error message. Indeed, the function will assign c a value of two times x. However, the calling program has no way of knowing what the value of c is. Remember, we're dealing with two separate programs here.

The following C language program will work just like the original BASIC program example. It is the correct C language version of this BASIC program:

```
main()
{

        int x;

        scanf("%d", &x);
        x = mult(x);
        printf("%d\n", x);

}
mult(c)
int c;
{

        c = c * 2;
        return(c)

}
```

This program does meet all of the necessary criteria to do what we originally wanted—that is, to multiply the value input at the keyboard by two. Within the function body, a return statement is used, and c is its argument. Just as we passed a value to the function from the calling program, it is necessary to pass a value from the function to the calling program. In BASIC, a RETURN statement is mandatory for a *proper* exit from a subroutine. In C, the return statement may be used with an argument to return a value to the calling program. It is sometimes used without an argument if a condition warrants the *premature* return from a function when an argument value is incorrect. However, a return statement is not mandatory to get out of a function. In C, the function will return control to the calling program when there are no more function lines to execute *or* when a return statement is encountered.

In the preceding program, the function will return a value that is equal to c. You will remember that c was used to represent the argument passed from the calling program. This value was then multiplied by two within the function body. Therefore, from the standpoint of value alone, c is equal to x * 2, which is what we wanted. When control is returned to the calling program, the function mult(x) will be equal to x * 2. This value is displayed on the screen by printf in the main body of the program.

The mult() function was called from the main program. This caused control to fall on the function. When the function finished executing, it returned control to the main program, along with a value that was the result of its operations.

The following C functions perform other types of mathematical operations:

```
sub(a, b)
int a, b;
{

    return(a - b);

}
```

****

```
add(a, b)
int a, b;
{

    return(a + b);

}
```

These simple functions subtract or add two integer values that are passed to them from the calling program. They might be used in the following manner:

```
main()
{

    int x, y;

    x = 10;
    y = 4;

    printf("%d   %d\n", sub(x, y), add(x, y));

}
/* This program body would be followed by the
   source code of the functions shown above */
```

This program calls the add() and sub() functions, which return the result of their mathematical operations to be used by printf.

It can be seen that functions allow often-used routines to be programmed only once, named, and then called by that name whenever they are needed. This not only speeds programming time, but it makes the C program far easier to understand. In BASIC, it would be necessary to track down various GOSUB branches to trace the flow of a program that operates similarly to the foregoing C example.

C functions can accept any legal argument, including char arrays and pointers to character strings. The following BASIC program will be converted to C to show how a function may manipulate string values:

```
10  A$="hello"
20  GOSUB 50
30  PRINT A$
40  END
50  A$=A$+"-goodbye"
60  RETURN
```

This program calls a subroutine to alter the value of A$. In C, this program could be written as follows:

```
main()
{

        char a[40];

        strcpy(a, "hello");

        alter(a);

        printf("%s\n", a);

}
alter(c)
char c[];
{
        strcat(c, "-goodbye");

}
```

In this example, the alter() function is used to add "-goodbye" to the end of its string argument. No return statement is necessary, because control will return to the calling program at the logical end of the function. We are not passing a value back to the function; instead, we are changing the value of a string already in memory. Notice that the argument to alter() is declared within the function as a char array. However, this declaration uses empty brackets where one would expect to find an integer constant specifying the number of elements or bytes.

This is not necessary when an array is passed to a function. Here, c[] is a pointer to the memory location of a in the calling program. This function could also have been written as follows:

```
alter(c)
char *c;
{

    strcat(c, "-goodbye");

}
```

since char arrays and char pointers may be interchanged in functions.

Instead of returning a value to the calling program, the alter() function changes the contents of the memory location assigned to the array. Since this memory location is also known by the calling program, no return is needed. This demonstrates the value of pointers in C. Don't be misled into thinking that this same procedure will work with standard numeric variables, as in the following:

```
main()
{

    int x;

    x = 14;

    alter(x);
                                    WRONG!!
    printf("%d\n", x);

}
alter(a)
int a;
{

    a = 24;

}
```

This will not change the value of x as seen by the calling program. The screen display from this example will be 14. The alter() function did nothing to change the value of x. Its variable a was assigned a value of 24, but the calling program has no contact with this variable or value, since it was not returned. Only pointer arguments allow functions to alter values in memory. All other types of arguments can be used only to return a value to the calling program.

Of course, it is quite easy to pass a pointer to a numeric quantity to a function. The following program is a proper modification of the last, incorrect example:

```
main()
{

    int x;

    x = 14;

    alter(&x);

    printf("%d\n", x);

}
alter(a)
int *a;
{

    *a = 24;

}
```

Here, the *address* of variable x in the main program is passed to alter(). Within the called function, a is declared a pointer to an integer. This is the memory location of the quantity stored in x. The memory location is assigned a value of 24 by the expression, *a = 24;. Control is then returned to the calling program, where the value of x is displayed on the monitor screen. The original value of x was 14, which was stored at the memory address set aside for x. However, the function was passed this memory address, as opposed to the *value* of x, and a new value was written at this location. When control is returned to the calling program, variable x is now equal to the new value stored at its memory location.

C LIKES INTEGERS BEST

The heading of this section should be a familiar concept. Again, C likes to assume that a quantity is an integer unless it is told otherwise. This especially applies to functions. C assumes that all functions return integer values, and an integer return is the default. However, if a function is to return a float, a double, a long, or even a pointer to a string, this noninteger return must be specially declared. As a matter of fact, it must be declared twice. As an example, functions such as log(), sqrt(), exp(), and the like, must be declared as doubles within the calling program. (*Note:* This does not apply to RUN/C.) These are functions that do not return integer values; they return doubles, and the calling program must be specifically instructed to expect this type of return. C also requires that a noninteger return be specified with the function name in the source code that makes up a function. The following program demonstrates this procedure:

```
main()
{

        double x, y, add();

        x = 14.1;
        y = 72.16;

        printf("%lf\n", add(x, y));

}
double add(a, b)
double a, b;
{

        return(a + b);

}
```

This is another version of the add() function discussed earlier; it accepts arguments that have been declared double and returns a double-precision value. In the calling program, add() is declared double. This alerts C to expect a double-precision return from add() instead of an integer. When the source code for the function is written, the name is preceded by double. Again, this is a signal that the function returns a double-precision value. Without these necessary declarations, the function will return an integer value to the calling program.

This rule applies for all other types of returns. If a function returns a long integer, then it must be declared long within the body of the calling program and preceding the function name. This is a requirement for all functions you may write. If such a function returns other than an integer, you must go through this declaration procedure.

BASIC FUNCTIONS IN C

Although the title of this section is a bit misleading, it is possible to write certain functions in C that will mimic the *operation* of useful BASIC functions. For instance, MID$, RIGHT$, and LEFT$ in BASIC must be translated as specialized functions in C, since this language does not contain their equivalents as part of its standard function set. These functions are not a standard part of C, so they must be specially programmed. All of these functions extract a portion of an argument string and write it to another array or return the extract value. The following function duplicates BASIC's LEFT$:

```
left$(a, b, x)
char *a, *b;
int x;
{
        int i;

        i = 0;

        while (i++ < x)
                *a++ = *b++;

        *a = '\0';

}
```

In this function, a and b are pointers to char arrays passed to left$(). Variable x represents the passed value of the number of characters to be extracted from the left side of the string. The passed string (actually, the address of the string) is represented by b, while a points to an array that will hold the result of left$().

Within the function, i is declared an int variable with an initial value of zero (0). A while loop reads each character in b to a and increments i by one on each pass. So long as i is less than the number of characters to be extracted, the loop continues to cycle. You must remember that x specifies the total number of characters. This means that character 1 is located at a[0], character 2 at a[1], and so on. If x is equal to 5, then the loop must count from 0 to 4. On each pass, both pointers are accessed for their character positions and then incremented to the next position. When the loop is exited, a points to a string of characters equal to the leftmost characters in b. However, this is not a true string yet, because the newly generated row of characters is not terminated by the required null byte. The last line in the function makes this assignment, and control is returned to the calling program.

SUMMARY

C language functions are quite easy to understand once you realize that they are separate miniprograms that are called from a master program or another function. They may receive arguments from the calling program and return values to it; or they may receive memory locations (pointers) as arguments and directly change the contents of these locations for use by the calling program.

Writing C functions is an excellent training aid. The exercise you gain from this practice will speed you along your course of proficiency in C. Fortunately, C language tutorials usually provide a wide assortment of specialized functions to learn from. All C functions follow the general format of standard C programs, so once you learn to write simple programs, you should also be able to write simple functions.

CHAPTER THREE

String Functions

The C language offers a small set of portable functions that perform many of the most common string manipulations. Each function works with a sequence of characters that is terminated by a null byte (0), which is the definition of a string in C. C strings and BASIC strings have many things in common, and some of the C functions used for string manipulation have direct equivalents in BASIC.

Strings and char arrays were presented briefly earlier in this text, but this chapter will delve more deeply into this subject and will explain each of the string utility functions found as part of the standard C language function set.

THE strcpy FUNCTION

The strcpy() function in C is the equivalent of the assignment operator (=) in BASIC when it is used to assign a value to a string variable. The following BASIC program:

$$10 \quad A\$ = "HELLO"$$

requires the strcpy() function when it is translated into C:

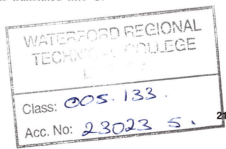

21

```
main()
{

    char a[10];

    strcpy(a, "HELLO");

}
```

A char array is declared, with ten sequential bytes set aside for storing a character string. This will allow for a string of a maximum of nine printable characters and a null byte to signal the end of the string. The constant "HELLO" is stored somewhere in memory. Strcpy() locates the first byte in "HELLO", which is the letter H, and copies it to the first storage location reserved for a. It then copies the second byte from the constant to the second storage position in a. This process continues until a null byte is copied. This terminates the strcpy() operation. The constant "HELLO" is stored by C as

H E L L O \0

When it is copied to the storage area reserved for a, the same sequence results. If you assume that the beginning storage location reserved for a is 100, then the sequence will be stored as

100	101	102	103	104	105	106	107	108	109
H	E	L	L	O	\0	**UNUSED	STORAGE**		

Actually, the characters are stored as one-byte integers with values of from 0 to 255, as in

100	101	102	103	104	105	106	107	108	109
72	69	76	76	79	0	**UNUSED	STORAGE**		

Each of the integer values is the ASCII code for the characters in "HELLO".
The following example uses two char arrays:

```
main()
{

    char a[10], b[10];

    strcpy(a, "HELLO");
    strcpy(b, a);

}
```

The first array is assigned the value of the constant "HELLO". Then strcpy() finds the storage location of the constant and copies it to the storage location set aside for a. Next, b is assigned the value of a, so the memory location of a is located and its contents are copied to the storage location for b. In each case, the source storage area is located and its contents copied to the target storage area.

Whenever a string value—be it a constant or contained in a char array—is to be assigned to a char array, the strcpy() function is used to handle this operation. The assignment operator (=) does not apply in such cases, as it does in BASIC or in C when numerical values are assigned to variables.

THE strlen FUNCTION

The strlen() function in C is equivalent to the LEN function in BASIC. Both return the total number of "printable characters" in a string. In C, the null character that terminates the string is not included as a part of the character count. The strlen() function counts all characters up to the null byte. Like LEN, strlen() always returns an integer value. The following BASIC program will serve as a demonstration:

```
10    A$="HELLO"
20    X%=LEN(A$)
30    PRINT X%
```

This program will display a value of 5 on the screen, because there are five characters in "HELLO". The C equivalent is

```
main()
{

    int x;
    char a[10];

    strcpy(a, "HELLO");

    x = len(a);

    printf("%d\n", x);

}
```

The same value is displayed by this program, since the value of "HELLO" in a contains five characters before the null byte.

In each of the previous examples, arrays have been declared for ten-character storage. C requires that *you* determine the size of the maximum string length any array can hold. In BASIC, string variables are usually fixed at a maximum length of

255 characters. This is quite wasteful of memory storage, since the unused storage areas are still assigned to the variable. In C, the size of a char array will be determined by the maximum length of a string this array might be asked to store. A value of 10 was chosen for the previous examples, because this was more than adequate to store "HELLO". Actually, a value of 6 would also be adequate, since "HELLO" will be stored in six bytes of memory (including the null byte).

THE strcat FUNCTION

BASIC allows strings to be added together in a mathematical way, as in

```
10   A$="PRO"
20   B$="GRAM"
30   A$=A$+B$
40   PRINT A$
```

This program displays the string "PROGRAM", which is the result of adding A$ and B$. We can't do this in C or in most other languages. Such an operation is found only in BASIC. However, C does offer a utility function called strcat() that can be used for this purpose. This function stands for *string concatenate*, which means to tack one string onto the end of another. The following program is a C language version of the preceding BASIC program:

```
main()
{

    char a[8], b[5];
    strcpy(a,  "PRO");
    strcpy(b,  "GRAM");

    strcat(a, b);

    printf("%s\n", a);

}
```

The arrays are declared with the absolute minimum of storage elements to properly effect the operation. Array a has eight elements and b has five. First, strcpy() is used to copy "PRO" to b. It is used again to copy "GRAM" to a. Then strcat() is called to copy the contents of b to the end of the string contained in a. After this call, a is equal to "PROGRAM". This is the value displayed on the screen.

The strcat() function uses the null byte in the destination string (a) to determine where the concatenation occurs. Originally, this null byte is located at array position 3, which is the point at which strcat() begins copying the contents of b. This function copies b up to and including the null byte. The end result is a properly terminated string that includes the original contents of a plus the contents of b.

Suppose you wished to add the values of several strings? The following BASIC program serves as an example:

```
10   A$="NEW "
20   B$="PRO"
30   C$="GRAM"
40   A$=A$+B$+C$
50   PRINT A$
```

This time, the string "NEW PROGRAM" is displayed. The first three characters are assigned to A$, the next three to B$, and the last four to C$. Variable A$ simply serves as a receptacle for the sum of B$ and C$. In C, this could be written as

```
main()
{

    char a[8], b[4], c[5]

    strcpy(a, "NEW ");
    strcpy(b, "PRO");
    strcpy(c, "GRAM");

    strcat(a, b);
    strcat(a, c);

    printf("%s\n", a);

}
```

It is necessary to use strcat() twice in this example. After the first call, a is equal to "NEW PRO". The second call to strcat() copies the contents of c onto the end of the previously concatenated contents of a.

THE sprintf FUNCTION

Besides the printf function, which has already been discussed, C also offers a version that writes a formatted output to a string pointer or char array instead of to the monitor screen. The following BASIC program can be duplicated in C using strcat(), but a more direct translation can be accomplished with sprintf:

```
10   B$="PRO"
20   C$="GRAM"
30   A$=B$+C$
40   PRINT A$
```

Here, A$ simply acts as a receptable for the sum of B$ and C$. The C version could be written as

```
main()
{

    char a[8], b[4], c[5];

    strcpy(b, "PRO");
    strcpy(c, "GRAM");

    sprintf(a, "%s%s", b, c);

    printf("%s\n", a);

}
```

The sprintf function writes its formatted output to the char array named as its first argument. This is followed by the control string, which indicates that two string values are expected. These two values are provided by arguments b and c, which follow the control string. When sprintf is executed, b and c are written as a single string to a. The sprintf line could also have been written as

```
sprintf(a, "%s   %s", b, c);
```

This would make a equal to "PRO   GRAM". The sprintf function works just like printf, in that the control string determines the exact format of the write. For instance:

```
sprintf(a, "%s%s", c, b);
```

would result in a being equal to "GRAMPRO". The sprintf function provides a great deal of flexibility in handling complex assignments to char arrays. It combines the traits of strcpy() and strcat() in a single function that may have a multitude of different arguments. It is also ideal for converting numeric values to string values, as in

```
sprintf(a, "%d %f %d", 14, 28.3, 32);
```

This results in a being equal to "14 28.3 32".

THE strcmp FUNCTION

The strcmp() function compares two string values and returns an integer value to indicate whether or not the strings match, whether the first is smaller than the second, or whether it is larger. In BASIC, we can use numeric operators such as =,

$<>$, $<=$, or $>=$ to compare two strings. In C, this type of string comparison requires the strcmp() function.

In most implementations, strcmp() will return a value of 0 if the strings are identical. If the two are not equal and the first unequal character in the first argument has a higher ASCII value than the same byte in the second string, a positive value is returned. If the byte in the first argument has a lower ASCII value than that in the second, a negative value is returned.

The strcmp() function is used in the following format:

$$x = strcmp(a, b);$$

where x is an int variable and a, b are pointers to char arrays or pointers to character strings. For example:

```
main()
{

        char a[10], b[10];
        int x;

        strcpy(a, "HELLO");
        strcpy(b, "HELLO");

        x = strcmp(a, b)

        printf("%d\n", x)

}
```

This program will display the value of 0 on the screen, because a is equal to b. If the value of a were changed to "hello", then x would be equal to a positive value, because the letter h has a higher ASCII value than H. If a were equal to "ARM", then a negative value would be returned to x. It's usually not necessary to know the exact values returned (other than 0 for a match), as the following program will demonstrate:

```
main()
{

    int x;
    char a[80], b[10];
    strcpy(b, "HELLO");

    gets(a);

    x = strcmp(a, b);

    if (x == 0)
        printf("The two are identical");
    else if (x < 0)
        printf("Smaller\n");
    else
        printf("Larger\n");

}
```

This program will indicate whether the string obtained from the keyboard is equal to, larger than, or smaller than "HELLO" on a byte-by-byte comparison.

SUMMARY

Although the standard set of string utility functions in C is small, most microcomputer implementations of C also offer additional functions that may be used to convert numbers to strings, to compare only a portion of character strings, and so forth. All of these functions probably use strcpy, strlen, sprintf, and strcmp as building blocks. With the basic string functions discussed in this chapter, hundreds of specialized functions that address string operations can be built. The standard set of string functions in C is small, but each is very powerful. Fortunately, too, their uses are quite easy to learn.

CHAPTER FOUR

Mathematical Functions

This chapter provides a discussion of C language functions that are designed to perform specific mathematical operations. Many of these represent functions that have become standard components of other high-level languages but, until a few years ago, have not normally been supplied with most C compilers. In recent years, many compilers have begun to offer what are known as the standard UNIX math functions, including sqrt(), pow(), sin(), cos(), and the like. Still, some inexpensive compilers do not offer these functions.

Whether your own compiler includes these functions or not, the discussion of the source programs that make up mathematical functions should be of benefit and should allow you to be better able to design personalized mathematical functions that are not currently addressed by any C language software.

You should also be aware that although mathematical function packages are available for C compilers, the algorithms used to develop each function may not be the most efficient possible. In other words, you may be able to write your own math functions that will execute faster than those included with some compilers and those offered as a part of optional mathematics packages for existing compilers.

To illustrate this point, a sqrt() function is discussed in this chapter that is a decided improvement over the one included as a part of the Lattice C/Microsoft C Compiler, Version 2.14. In benchmark testing, the sqrt() function was called 1000 times consecutively on an IBM Personal Computer equipped with an 8087 math coprocessor. The commercial version of this function required 46 seconds to make the calls, whereas the version of this same function discussed in this chapter took only 14 seconds.

Many universal formulas that have been used for decades to approximate mathematical operations can be made more efficient (speeded up) by making the proper additions or modifications for custom-tailoring algorithms to a particular language. To do this, it is necessary to understand the language itself, especially in regard to the type of operations that tend to execute faster. Naturally, integer operations will execute faster than those that require floating point math. Sometimes, however, it is possible to modify floating point formulas in such a manner that integer mathematics can be used, at least for a major portion of the operation.

It should be understood that I am by no means a mathematical expert. All of the programs presented here were derived from reading mathematical texts, especially compendiums of mathematical formulas. Admittedly, many of the formulas obtained were not directly practical for inclusion in computer programs, but each served as a basis for devising a method by which a modification of the formula could be developed that would produce accuracy with execution efficiency.

I think you will find the mathematical examples discussed in this chapter educational as well as immediately useful when they are incorporated as part of your working function set. Each program is presented with an emphasis on clarity of content and with the beginner in mind. This, coupled with the discussion of each program, should make clear the operation of each function line. It is hoped that this style of presentation will help you begin designing the specialized mathematical functions needed more and more in modern computer applications.

THE bin2dec FUNCTION

The conversion of 8-bit binary numbers to their decimal equivalents is not a difficult procedure, but it makes an interesting introductory study for writing mathematical functions in C. Such an operation is often useful in developing more complex functions, many of which address the programming of graphics applications.

The conversion of binary numbers to their decimal equivalencies requires accessing each data bit in descending positional order (7 to 0 for 8-bit numbers) and, if the bit is on, raising the value of 2 to the power of its bit position.

```
bin2dec(bin)
char bin[];
{

    int dec, x;

    dec = 0;

    for (x = 7; x >= 0; --x)
        if (bin[7 - x] != '0')
            dec += raise(x);

    return(dec);

}
```

```
raise(x)
int x;
{

    int inc, p;

    p = 1;

    for (inc = 1; inc <= x; ++inc)
        p *= 2;

    return(p);

}
```

The bin2dec function is passed a character string value that represents the binary number as bits of either 1 or 0. This is contained in bin. Within the function, two int variables are declared, dec and x. The first will later be returned as the decimal equivalent of bin. The second int variable is decremented from 7 to 0 in the for loop. On each pass, the if statement line checks the characters in ascending array positions, testing for a value other than 0 or, more specifically, the number 1. When a 1 is encountered, dec is incremented by a second function I have arbitrarily named raise(). This is a modification of the power function used to raise integers to integer powers. However, raise() is intended specifically for the purpose of raising 2 to the power of x. Therefore, this may be thought of as a specialized function intended to be called solely by bin2dec.

The value of x is passed to raise(). Remember, this variable contains the value of the bit position being accessed. The return value (p) is the decimal value of 2 raised to the power x. Back in the original function, dec is incremented by this value.

When all bit positions have been accessed, the value of dec will be equal to the decimal equivalent of bin, and this value is returned to the calling program. I could just as easily have dropped the separate raise function and included its program lines within the body of bin2dec; however this two-function approach may make the explanation a bit clearer. Execution speed will be faster by omitting a second function call, but since both functions deal with integer values, any speed increase will probably be minor in almost every application.

The following program illustrates the use of bin2dec:

```
main()
{

        char *a;
        int i;

        a = "11110000";
        x = bin2dec(a);

        printf("%d\n", x);

}
```

This program will print the decimal equivalent of binary 11110000, or 240 in decimal.

Of course, there are many other ways of writing this same function. If the addition of the raise() function is troubling to you, either from a point of understanding the bin2dec function or from the standpoint of execution speed, it can be omitted completely. Examining the function and, more specifically, its impact on bin2dec, we can see that it will always return an even dividend of 128. If we assume that the binary quantity passed to bin2dec contains all ''on'' bits (that is, 11111111), then raise() will return the values 128, 64, 32, 16, 8, 4, 2, 1 as it is accessed from bin2dec. Remember, raise() is called only when the bit is equal to 1.

Knowing this, we can rewrite the bin2dec function in the following way:

```
bin2dec(bin)
char bin[];
{

        int a, dec, x;

        a = 128;
        dec = 0;

        for (x = 7; x >= 0; --x) {
                if (bin[7 - x] != '0')
                        dec += a;

                a /= 2;
        }

        return(dec);

}
```

In this example, raise() is deleted and replaced with a simple routine that divides variable a by two on each pass of the x loop. This still gives us the appropriate value of 2 raised to the bit position power, but it does so in a more efficient manner. This function is to be preferred over the first example, which was discussed only to give the reader a basis in the theory behind such conversions. The first function follows the formula for binary to decimal conversion as it would be displayed mathematically. The second function incorporates a "shorthand" method of arriving at the same return values but in a more efficient manner. Faster execution is the end result.

THE dec2bin FUNCTION

The conversion of binary to decimal is a quite common exercise addressed by computer programs; however, the reverse conversion is not seen as often. The dec2bin function is used to convert a decimal integer value to its 8-bit binary equivalent. It is the reverse of the bin2dec function but uses some of the same routines to achieve its results.

```
dec2bin(c, x)
char c[];
int x;
{
        int a, ct;

        a = 128;
        ct = 0;

        while ( a >= 1) {
                if ((x - a) >= 0) {
                        c[ct++] = '1';
                        x -= a;
                }
                else
                        c[ct++] = '0';

                a /= 2;
        }


        c[ct] = '\0';

}
```

To convert a decimal integer to its 8-bit binary equivalent, it is necessary to subtract the values 128, 64, 32, 16, 8, 4, 2, and 1, respectively. You will remember that these values represent 2 raised to the power of each bit position (7 to 0). So long as the difference is 0 or greater, the respective bit position is "on" (equal to 1). If a negative value is the result, then the bit position is off (equal to 0).

To demonstrate this, the following mathematical sequence will convert the decimal quantity 221 to its binary equivalent:

```
221 - 128 =  93  Bit position = 1
 93 -  64 =  29  Bit position = 1
 29 -  32 =  -3  Bit position = 0
 29 -  16 =  13  Bit position = 1
 13 -   8 =   5  Bit position = 1
  5 -   4 =   1  Bit position = 1
  1 -   2 =  -1  Bit position = 0
  1 -   1 =   0  Bit position = 1

Decimal 221 = Binary 11011101
```

This function reflects this mathematical sequence and assigns the binary equivalent of its passed argument to char array c[]. As with the bin2dec function, a simple routine is set up to decrement int variable a in steps of one-half its previous value. On each pass of the while loop, the array position of c[] is incremented by 1. The if statement line tests for a value of 0 or more after the subtraction has taken place. If this is true, then the current array position is assigned a value of 1. Notice that this is a char, not the integer 1. If the if test proves false, else takes over and the array position is assigned a value of 0. In either situation, ct is incremented by 1. The final step of this function before returning control to the calling program is to assign the last position in c[] the null terminator ('\0'). This is required to detect the end of a char string.

BASIC MATH FUNCTIONS

It seems that every C language add-on library package contains a set of basic math functions, often including add(), sub(), mult(), and div(). As their names imply, these functions are used to add, subtract, multiply, or divide two arguments. Some of them are even broken down into separate functions that add integers or add floating point numbers, for instance. I question the utility of these types of functions, since it is far easier to type

$$x = a + b;$$

in a C language program than it is to type

```
x = add(a, b);
```

I suspect that such functions are often included with such software packages simply
to increase the total number of function that are advertised for these products. Here
are some versions of these functions:

```
add(a, b)
int a, b;
{

        return(a + b);
}
sub(a, b)
int a, b;
{

        return(a - b);

}
mult(a, b)
int a, b;
{

        return(a * b);

}
double div(a, b)
double a, b;
{

        return(a / b);

}
```

All but the last function use integer arguments and returns. Owing to the nature of
div(), it almost always uses floating point arguments and returns.

The problem with all of these functions lies in the fact that the argument types
must be declared as well as the returns. This means that a function that accepts int
arguments cannot be used to perform the same mathematical operation on floats or
doubles.

To overcome this, most implementations of these operations are handled
through macro definitions. The nice thing about macros of this type is that they will

handle any numeric data type. The same four operations handled above as functions may be written as macros in the following manner:

```
#define add(A, B)      (A + B)
#define sub(A, B)      (A - B)
#define mult(A, B)     (A * B)
#define div(A, B)      (A / B)
```

With macros, it really doesn't matter what types of arguments are supplied in these examples; therefore, add() will work just as well with double arguments as it will with those that have been declared ints, shorts, longs, or floats. A macro definition is a preprocessor command. Basically, a macro is provided at the head of a program and before main() is called. During the compilation process, the macro definition line is substituted into the program anywhere a macro call is made. If a C program is written with a macro definition, as in

```
#define add(A, B)    (A + B)
main()
{

    printf("%d\n", add(1, 4));

}
```

the program that is actually compiled would be

```
main()
{

    printf("%d\n", (1 + 4));

}
```

The macro is add(A, B). The macro definition is (A + B). Therefore (A + B) is substituted for add(A, B) when the program is compiled.

Macros can be used to good advantage in some programming situations, especially where it is desirable to pass arguments of different numeric data types for some mathematical operation.

COMPLEX FUNCTIONS

To this point, all functions have involved reasonably simple mathematical formulas and operations, although a few new twists have been presented. Each example was presented merely to set the stage for what is to follow. This section will deal with the mathematical functions most needed by the general programmer. Each of these complex functions can be put to use in many different programming environments.

As we move on to functions that return various roots of numbers or raise numbers to fractional powers, a new area of mathematics is required. Most functions of this nature depend on *approximations*. Approximations are formulas, but they are often more limited than what we usually think of as true formulas. For instance, the simple formula

$$A = X + Y$$

will always work in a program or function, regardless of the values used for X and for Y (assuming that these values are within the range your computer can handle). However, a formula that is used to represent an approximation may not feature this universal nature regarding values. The arguments that are fed to an approximation often must fall within a certain value range for a proper output. Many approximations that deal with the complex subject of exponentiation require an argument that is more than 0 but less than 1. Since it is usually desirable to use such approximations for a far wider range of values in practical applications, it is often necessary to perform conversions on the input argument to make it fit the limited range. Once the answer is output, an extrapolation process must be performed for a conversion that reflects the true input argument. It is for this reason that many of the approximations you will find in mathematical texts will require considerable modification when they are written into a practical computer program.

The functions discussed in this section are the result of hundreds of hours of independent study and experimentation, using basic approximations as a start. Some of the functions were finally derived from a long series of hit-and-miss experiments. Some were the subject of week-long concentrated efforts that ended in complete failure, only to have the proper procedure seemingly pop up from obvious oversights that were suddenly discovered. Adding to this ordeal was the constant problem of efficiency or execution time. Once a workable procedure was obtained, it was then usually necessary to fine-tune the function to speed it up. This process often required more time (and function lines) than the basic procedure did. In the end, however, all functions presented here performed as intended. A later section rates each one.

Writing complex mathematical functions is certainly within the grasp of any programmer who has a reasonable basis in algebra, geometry, and trigonometry. If I had a degree in mathematics, the many hours spent on this project would certainly have been reduced to a fraction of the original. However, I present myself as an individual with an average mathematical background, who has had standard high school and college mathematics and who has probably forgotten 60 percent of what he once knew on the subject. This seems to be an appropriate background to relate how average programmers might wish to proceed in writing mathematical functions.

The sqrt Function

One of the first complex functions that is often attempted by programmers is one that will return the square root of a number. My first stab at this involved a complicated progression series that simply squared low integer values until the result was more than the number whose root was to be taken. The program then subtracted 1 from the number that had been squared and began adding values to this integer in increments of 0.1. These numbers were squared and checked against the original argument. This process was repeated over and over, using progressively smaller increments (.01, .001, .0001, and so forth). When the root squared was equal to or within a very small fraction of the argument, the square root was returned to the calling program.

Although this worked quite well, the function took forever to return a value; the process was much too cumbersome. The program simply tried a progressive series of numbers until the square of one number equaled the number whose root was to be taken. We've all probably done this from time to time using paper and pencil. The computer speeds up the operation, but it's still slow in terms of good mathematical functions.

Finally, I discovered *Newton's approximation* in a text of mathematical formulas. It seemed to be and, indeed, was the answer to my prayers. Before going further, it is necessary to make certain the reader is aware of the terms that will be used in discussions of functions that return a specific root of a value.

The following table is provided to aid in understanding future explanations:

$$5 = \text{square root of } 25$$
$$\text{or}$$
$$5 = 2 \text{ root of } 25$$

Root = 5
Radicand = 25
Index = 2

$$2 = \text{4th root of } 16$$

Root = 2
Radicand = 16
Index = 4

The number whose root is to be taken is the *radicand;* the *index* names the root to be taken; and the *root* is the value of the index of the radicand.

Newton's approximation reads:

$$\text{ROOT} = 1/n * ((r/aprox) + (n - 1) * aprox)$$

where *n* is the index, *r* is the radicand, and *aprox* is an approximation of the final root value. Therefore, the square root of a value is determined by

$$\text{SQRT} = 1/2((r/aprox) + (2 - 1) * aprox)$$

or

$$\text{SQRT} = ((r/aprox) + aprox)/ 2)$$

Naturally, the first question usually asked pertains to *aprox*. After all, if you have to provide an approximation of the square root of *x*, in order to arrive at Newton's approximation of the square root of *x*, what good is the whole thing anyway? This is a very good question, but the fact is that you can use any reasonable value for *aprox*. I have found that assigning a value of one-half the value of the radicand works just fine. You could also use the whole value of that number, but the closer you come to the actual square root value in your approximation, the faster a C function using this formula works. If the radicand is less than 1, don't halve this value for *aprox;* simply use the value as is.

The following function shows how Newton's approximation is used to produce sqrt() in C:

```
#define  abs(T)   (T < 0) ? -T : T
double sqrt(b)   /* Return the square root of b */
double b;
{

     double x, y;

     b = abs(b);

     y = b / 2; /* Root approximation */
     x = b * 2;

     while (abs(x - y) > .0000001) {
          x = y;
          y = ((b / y) + y) / 2; /* Calculate root */
     }

     return(y);

}
```

This function is declared double, since square roots most usually result in floating point values. Even if the root is a whole number (that is, the square root of 4), it will be returned as a double. A macro is defined at the beginning of the function to return the absolute value of the radicand. This avoids hang-ups if a negative value is ever passed to this function. The square root of a negative value is an imaginary number; therefore, any negative number that is passed to sqrt() is automatically converted to its absolute value, which is always positive.

It is perfectly correct to #define a macro as a part of a function, so long as the function is to be included with a C language program. However, if such functions are to be compiled separately, presumably to be converted to a library module called from a linker, the macro definition must be defined at the beginning of the calling program.

In this function, variable b is the radicand. It is declared double, as are internal variables x and y. The abs macro assures that a positive value is passed on to the rest of the function, and then variable y is assigned a value of b/2. This will serve as the approximation to be worked through Newton's formula. Variable x is initially assigned a value of b * 2. This variable will be used to test for the desired root value in order to exit from the while loop that follows.

Newton's approximation is contained within the body of the loop. The loop continues to cycle so long as the difference between x and y is greater than 0.0000001. The difference is processed through abs() to assure a positive value for this test.

Newton's approximation works easily in computer programs, even though a very crude approximation of the final answer is initially provided. (*Note:* "Crude approximation" refers to the radicand divided by 2, *not* to the final return value from this function.) This is so because each time the formula outputs an answer, it is substituted as a new approximation and the formula is worked again. On each loop cycle, the approximation gets closer to the correct value (the square root of the radicand), until the true root is actually obtained or a repetition is set up where two different values are output from the formula, each being within 0.0000001 of the other. Either condition signals for loop termination, and the value of y is returned as the square root.

Looking at the contents of the loop, we see that y is calculated on each pass on the basis of its initial value as worked through the formula. The new value of y is fed back into the formula and recalculation occurs. On each loop pass, x is assigned the value of y before the formula is worked. When x = y or differs from it by ±0.0000001, the final square root value is obtained.

The cubrt Function

Newton's approximation also works very well in taking other indices. The only limitation is that all indices must be integer values. In other words, we can take the cube root of a number as easily as we can take the square root. The cubrt function demonstrates this:

```
#define abs(T)   (T < 0) ? -T : T
double cubrt(x)   /* Return cube root of x */
double x;
{

    double a, b;


    a = x / 3;   /* Root approximation */

    b = 2 * x;

    while (abs(b - a) > .0000001) {

        b = a;

        a = ((x / (a * a)) + (2 * a)) / 3;

    }



    return(a);



}
```

This function follows the same principles as sqrt(); however, the formula has been changed to reflect the desired return of the cube root. The initial approximation assignment to variable a is now the radicand divided by 3. The remainder of the function works in the same manner described for sqrt().

Better Root Functions

The two functions just described are excellent in terms of accuracy, but they leave quite a bit to be desired from the standpoint of execution speed. As presented, each will require approximately 45 to 50 seconds to handle 1000 successive calls from a C program (assuming use of an IBM PC with 8087 math coprocessor). Execution time is directly affected by the value of the radicand and, more important, by the quality of the initial approximation that is worked through the formula. For example, taking the square root of 4 is extremely rapid, because our starting approximation is 4/2, or 2. Since 2 is the square root of 4, this approximation value is worked through the formula only once before the return value is obtained. However, the square root of 8 takes a bit longer, because 8/2 is 4. This approximation must be worked through the formula more times before the correct return value is calculated.

In experimenting with Newton's approximation, I quickly discovered that its efficiency is highly dependent on the quality of the initial approximation value. The closer this approximation is to the actual square (or cube) root, the fewer times it is necessary to work through the formula.

In order to speed up sqrt() and cubrt(), it is necessary to develop some routine that can better approximate a starting value. To begin with, we know that computers handle integer math much more rapidly than floating point operations. The root functions presented so far, out of necessity, depend entirely on floating point operations. However, it might be possible to rewrite these functions to return the integer square root or cube root of a number. Although this probably would not be useful as a final return value, it would be a far better first approximation of the same root to be worked through our present floating point function. Obviously, it will take only a short execution time to arrive at the integer square or cube root, and perhaps this time could be more than made up for by an increase in efficiency within the floating point phase because of a better initial approximation.

The following function uses all of these ideas to form a very efficient square root function:

```
#define   abs(T)    (T < 0) ? -T : T
double sqrt(b)    /* Return the square root of b */
double b;
{

     double x, y;
     long aprox();

     b = abs(b);

     y = (b > 1) ? (double) aprox(b) : b;   /* Approximation */
     x = b * 2;

     while (abs(x - y) > .0000001) {
          x = y;
          y = ((b / y) + y) / 2; /* Calculate root */
     }

     return(y);

}
long aprox(f)    /* Return integer approximation */
double f;
{

     long a, b, x;
```

```
x = f;   /* Convert f to long */
a = x;
b = 2 * x;

while (b - a > 0) {
      b = a;
      a = ((x / a) + a) / 2;
}

return(a);

}
```

This function appears very similar to the earlier version of sqrt(), but a new function, called aprox(), has been tacked to the end of it. If you examine the two functions carefully, you will see that aprox() is an integer version of sqrt(). The first function calls the second; therefore, a call to sqrt() from a C language program also results in a call to aprox(). The latter function is declared a long, because the mathematics involved in working through the integer version of the Newtonian formula often results in long integers. This is true even though the final return value will usually be a standard integer value.

The function aprox() is called early in this function, as this is the point in the earlier version of sqrt() where the radicand was simply divided by 2. The value returned from aprox() is assigned to variable y, assuming that the radicand argument is more than 1. If it is less than 1, aprox() is not called, since such a quantity would revert to integer 0. A cast operator is used to convert the long return from aprox() to double, as this is the point in the function where the floating point phase begins.

At this stage of execution, variable y is now equal to the integer square root of the radicand. This is a much closer approximation than can be obtained from simply dividing the radicand by 2. Obtaining the integer approximation costs very little in execution time, because integer math is handled much more efficiently by the computer. The floating point portion of this complex function will also be more efficient, because the more accurate approximation means that the formula will not be worked through as many times.

Comparison tests between the first version of sqrt() and this one prove the increased efficiency. On an IBM Personal Computer equipped with an 8087 math coprocessor, 1000 calls to the first version required approximately 50 seconds. The second version of sqrt() required only 14 seconds to make the same number of calls. Both test programs were compiled with the Lattice C compiler, Version 2.14. Thus, the modified version of sqrt() ran about three and one-half times faster. This is quite a step in efficiency.

If obtaining an integer approximation improves the performance of sqrt(), then surely it must do the same for cubrt(). Since both functions use Newton's approximation, cubrt() should, and does, perform about three and one-half times faster when written in the following manner:

```
#define abs(T)    (T < 0) ? -T : T
double cubrt(x)   /* Return cube root of x */
double x;
{

     double a, b;
     int sign;
     long aprox();

     sign = (x > 0) ? 1 : -1;
     x = abs(x);

     a = (x > 1) ? (double) aprox(x) : x;   /* Approximation */

     b = 2 * x;

     while (abs(b - a) > .0000001) {
          b = a;
          a = ((x / (a * a)) + (2 * a)) / 3;
     }

     return(sign * a);

}
long aprox(f)    /* Return integer approximation */
double f;
{

     long a, b, x;

     x = f;  /* Convert f to long */
     a = x;
     b = 2 * x;

     while (b - a > 0) {
          b = a;
          a = ((x / (a * a)) + (2 * a)) / 3;
     }

     return(a);

}
```

The explanation for this function is nearly identical to that for the previous one. Here, aprox() is the long integer equivalent of cubrt(). In both versions of this function, the variable sign multiplied by a (the absolute cube root value) is returned. Unlike square roots, cube roots can be either positive or negative values. If the radicand argument passed to cubrt() is negative, sign equals -1, thus producing a negative return. If not, sign is equal to 1. The abs() macro converts the argument to a positive value (if necessary) *after* variable sign has been assigned a value of ± 1. Using the same techniques, functions can easily be written that will return the fourth, fifth, sixth, and so on, root of any number. All that is necessary is to program the proper version of Newton's approximation.

The following function, called root(), will return the specified root of a number, so long as the index is an integer. In other words, it can be used to take the fourth root, for instance, but not the 4.5th root. The function is written as follows:

```
#define abs(T)   (T < 0 ) ? -T : T
double root(x, pw)   /* Return pw root of x */
double x;

int pw;
{

        double a, b, r;
        int i, p, sign;

        if (pw == 0)   /* Root zero */
              return(1);

        if (pw == 1)   /* Root 1 */
              return(x);

        if (pw == -1)   /*Root -1 */
              return(1 / x);

        p = abs(pw);

        sign = (x < 0  && p % 2 != 0) ? -1 : 1;   /* Set sign */

        p -= 1;
        x = abs(x);
        a = x / 2;
        b = 2 * x;

        while (abs(b - a) > .0000001) {
              b = a;
              r = 1;

              for (i = 1; i <= p; ++i)
                    r *= a;   /* r == a to the p power */

              a = ((x / r) + (p * a)) / (p + 1);   /* Get root */
        }

        return((pw > 0) ? sign * a : sign * 1 / a);

}
```

This function represents a simple modification of the original sqrt() and cubrt() functions discussed earlier. It accepts two arguments: the radicand and the index. The radicand argument is declared double, and the index must be an integer.

To test for indices of 0, 1, or − 1, three if statement lines are used. The 0 root of any number is 1, the 1 root is the radicand itself, and the − 1 root is the radicand divided into 1.

Assuming that other values are passed to this function, the same routine is set up as before, using Newton's approximation. This is the basic version of root(), so the initial approximation is obtained by dividing the radicand by 2. Within the while loop, p—the absolute radicand value—is inserted into the formula. Earlier, variable sign was set to either 1 or − 1, depending on whether the radicand was positive or negative. If it was negative and was to be taken to an even-numbered index, then sign was necessarily equal to 1, since an irrational value results when a negative number is taken to an even-numbered root. Therefore, the square root of − 10 will be the same as the square root of + 10 with this function. When the radicand value is negative and the index is an odd value, sign is equal to − 1.

In the event of a negative index—such as root(10.0, − 2.0)—the return statement returns the value derived from the formula divided into 1. This follows the proper mathematical procedure for negative indices (for example, the − 4 root of x = the 4th root of x divided into 1).

Within the while loop, there is a version of Kernighan and Ritchie's power() function. This function raises a floating point number to an integer power, which is one of the necessary steps in working through the Newtonian approximation. Previously, sqrt() and cubrt() did not require this routine (set up by the for loop) since the indices were fixed.

The root function lends itself well to the speed-up procedure discussed earlier. The following function uses aprox() to return a far more accurate initial approximation to root():

```
#define abs(T)   (T < 0 ) ? -T : T
double root(x, pw)   /* Return pw root of x */
double x;
int pw;
{
        double a, b, r;
        int i, p, sign;
        long aprox();

        if (pw == 0)   /* Root zero */
                return(1);

        if (pw == 1)   /* Root 1 */
                return(x);

        if (pw == -1)   /*Root -1 */
                return(1 / x);

        p = abs(pw);
```

```
    sign = (x < 0  && p % 2 != 0) ? -1 : 1;   /* Set sign */

    p -= 1;
    x = abs(x);
    a = (x > 1) ? (double) aprox(x, p) : x; /*Approximation */
    b = 2 * x;

    while (abs(b - a) > .0000001) {
        b = a;
        r = 1;

        for (i = 1; i <= p; ++i)
            r *= a;  /* r == a to the p power */

        a = ((x / r) + (p * a)) / (p + 1);   /* Get root */
    }

    return((pw > 0) ? sign * a : sign * 1 / a);
}
long aprox(f, p) /* Return integer approximation */
double f;
int p;
{
    long a, b, r, x;
    int i;

    x = f;  /* Convert f to long */
    a = x;
    b = 2 * x;

    while (b - a > 0) {
        b = a;
        r = 1;

        for (i = 1; i <= p; ++i)
            r *= a;   /* r == a to the p power */

        a = ((x / r) + (p * a)) / (p + 1);
    }

    return(a);

}
```

As before, aprox() is a long integer version of root() and returns the initial approximation to be worked through the formula. The return value is a long integer, but it is converted to double by the cast operator upon return to the calling function, root(). You will find that root() works a bit more slowly than discrete functions like sqrt(), but because of aprox(), it is still quite fast and is suitable for many different programming environments.

The log, exp, and pwr Functions

Although the root functions are highly useful in many mathematical operations, more functions are required to have a complete set of mathematical tools for general programming operations. We will certainly need a function by which values can be raised to any power. Kernighan and Ritchie presented a function called power(), but it could only be used to raise values to integer powers.

The complex functions discussed to this point effectively raise values to noninteger powers. The sqrt() function raises its argument to the 1/2 power, and cubrt() raises to the 1/3 power. Another function, root(), was used to allow the index or power to be specified in a passed argument, but it is still limited to integer indices. This function is fine when it is desired, for instance, to raise 3.1 to the 1/4 power. The index in this example would be 4. This is the same as taking 3.1 to the power of 0.250. However, if we wished to raise 3.1 to the power 0.265, root() would not be capable of doing the job.

What is needed is a function that can accept any argument as a power to which a value is to be raised. One method for accomplishing this is through the formula

$$a = \exp(y * \log (x))$$

where a is the result of raising x to the y power.

This formula means that it is necessary to write two new functions that can return natural logarithms and exponents. These two functions will then be combined to produce a truly versatile power function.

log.   There are many approximations available for determining logarithms. Unfortunately, most of them are very limited in the range of values that can be worked through them. For the log function discussed here, I chose to use a polynomial approximation I obtained from a textbook. It actually approximates logarithms to the base 10, as opposed to natural logarithms, but a simple and quick conversion is all that is necessary to arrive at the desired natural logarithm.

This approximation was chosen because it was simple and would execute quickly within the body of a C function. Initial experimentation made it clear, however, that its accuracy suffered whenever logarithms were derived from argument values that were less than 1 or more than 2. Fortunately, it is quite easy to modify the initial argument so that it will fall between 1 and 2. This modified value is worked through the formula; then multipliers act on the output value to return the logarithm of the original argument. For instance:

$$\log(x) = = (\log(1 / x) * -1)$$

and

$$\log(x) = = (\log(\text{sqrt}(x)) * 2)$$

The first conversion is used if *x* is too small. The logarithm is calculated from the reciprocal of the argument and then converted to the actual logarithm by multiplying the output by − 1. If an argument is too large, the log can be calculated from the square root (or other roots) and the output converted by multiplying it by the root index.

The log function uses these conversions to achieve the best accuracy possible from the polynomial approximation:

```
double log(x)      /*Return natural logarithm of x */
double x;
{
     int ct, lt;
     double t, y, sqrt();

     ct = lt = 1;

     if (x < 1) {
          x = 1 / x;      /* Raise x to the -1 power */
          lt = -1;        /* Set return multiplier */
     }

     while (x > 2) {
          x = sqrt(x);    /* take sqrt of x until <= 2 */
          ct *= 2;        /* Log multiplier */
     }

/* Derive log(x) through polynomial approximation */
     t = (x - 1) / (x + 1);
     y = .868591718 * t;
     y = y + .289335524 * (t * t * t);
     y = y + .177522071 * (t * t * t * t * t);
     y = y + .094376476 * (t * t * t * t * t * t * t);
     y = y + .179337714 * ( t * t * t * t * t * t * t * t * t);

/* Divide by log10(e) and multiply by ct and lt
   for natural logarithm */

     return(y / .43429446 * ct *lt);

}
```

This function accepts a double argument, so if integer constants are to be passed, you must make certain that they are converted to floating point format (for example, 12 = 12.0). Two integer variables are declared internally. These will serve as conversion multipliers. Two internal double variables, t and y, are worked through the approximation formula. Notice that sqrt() is also declared a double. The calling program or function must be alerted to functions that return other than integer values. It is assumed that sqrt() will be included with this function or with the program calling it. The efficient version of sqrt() discussed earlier is preferred for fastest execution time.

Initially, int variables ct and lt are set to values of + 1. The if statement tests the value of the argument and makes the necessary conversions to allow the calculation to be based on a value between 1 and 2. As an example, assume that the argument (*x*) is 0.25. The if statement detects that this value is less than 1; therefore, x is converted to its reciprocal (1 / x), or 4.0. The multiplier, lt, is assigned a new value of − 1. Next, the while loop is entered. Since x is now equal to 4.0, the test proves true (x > 2), so sqrt() is called. This returns the value of 2.0 [sqrt (4.0) = 2.0], and variable ct is incremented to 2. This causes an exit from the loop. (If the value returned from sqrt() was still larger than two, the loop would cycle again and sqrt() would return the square root of its previous return. Variable ct would then be incremented to 4.)

At this point, the polynomial approximation formula is worked. At its conclusion, variable y is equal to the logarithm to the base 10 of 2.0. However, you will recall that the desired output is the *natural* logarithm of .250. The return statement contains the needed conversion, which first divides y by a fixed quantity— log10(e). This quantity never changes. The result is then multiplied by ct and by lt, respectively. The final result is the natural logarithm of 0.250.

The conversion formula can be stated as follows:

$$\log(0.250) = (\log 10(2.0) \, / \, .43429446 * 2 * \, -1)$$

These are the steps log() goes through to return the natural logarithm of 0.250.

This function executes rapidly, but it is also dependent on the execution speed of sqrt(). A poor sqrt function will greatly decrease its efficiency.

If you desire a function that will return logarithms to the base 10, simply change the return statement to

```
return( y * ct * lt);
```

The log function is extremely fast, requiring about eight seconds for 1000 calls (on an IBM PC with an 8087 coprocessor); however, this high speed is paid for at the sacrifice of accuracy. The formula used results in accuracy to at least the fifth decimal place. For many applications, this will certainly be adequate, but others may require a higher precision.

The following version of log() works more slowly, but its accuracy is good to about eight decimal places. This version uses a different (and longer) approximation; 1000 calls to this function will require approximately 34 seconds, or twice the access time of the previous function:

```
double log(x)     /*Return natural logarithm of x */
double x;
{

     int ct, lt;
     double t, y;
```

```
ct = lt = 0;

while (x < 1) {
     x *= 10;
     ++lt;
}

while (x > 2.0) {
     x /= 2.0;
     ++ct;
}
```

```
/* Derive log(x) through polynomial approximation */
```

```
t = x - 1;
y = .9999964239 * t;
y = y + -.4998741238 * t * t;
y = y + .3317990258 * t * t * t;
y = y + -.2407338084 * t * t * t * t;
y = y + .1676540711 * t * t * t * t * t;
y = y + -.0953293897 * t * t * t * t * t * t;
y = y + .0360884937 * t * t * t * t * t * t * t;
y = y + -.0064535442 * t * t * t * t * t * t * t * t;
```

```
return(y + (ct * 0.6931471805599453) - (lt * 2.3025850929940457));
```

```
}
```

The approximation used in this function outputs the natural logarithm of 1 plus its argument. The argument must be a value between and including 0 and 1. The same multiplication and division processes as those discussed with the previous function take place before a value is passed to the approximation routine. The idea is to convert the original argument to a value of more than or equal to 1 and less than or equal to 2—the minimum and maximum values that may be fed to the approximation routine.

A value of 1 is subtracted from the modified value of the argument. This is necessary because this approximation routine returns the logarithm of 1 plus its argument. Therefore, if the argument is modified to a value of 1.5, this is also equal to log(1 + .5).

The output from the approximation is added to the logarithm of 2 times the value of ct. This variable counts the number of times the argument was divided by 2. The sum is then reduced by lt times the logarithm of 10. Variable lt has a value equal to the number of times the original argument was multiplied by 10.

The final return value is a more precise logarithm of the argument, usually accurate to at least eight decimal places. This increased accuracy can be quite important, especially when log() is used to return a value for other functions.

exp. With the completion of log(), we are at the halfway point in building the functions necessary to arrive at a good power function. The next tool needed is a function that will return the exponential value of an argument. The exponential value of x is equal to:

$$e\hat{\ }x$$

where $e = 2.718281828459045$.

The following C function returns the exponential value of its argument:

```
double exp(b)         /* Return e raised to the b power */
                      /* Accurate when b ranges from -10 to 10 */
double b;
{

        int ct, i;
        double x, y, z;

        x = (b < 0) ? -b : b;   /* Get abs b */
        ct = y = z = 1;

        while (x >= 1) {
             x /= 2;   /* Divide x by 2 */
             ct *= 2;  /* Return multiplier */
        }

/* Exponential approximation */

        y += -.9999999995 * x;
        y += .4999999206 * x * x;
        y += -.1666653019 * x * x * x;
        y += .0416573475 * x * x * x * x;
        y += -.0083013598 * x * x * x * x * x;
        y += .0013298820 * x * x * x * x * x * x;
        y += -.0001413161 * x * x * x * x * x * x * x;

        y = (b < 0) ? y : 1 / y;   /* Determine final value */

        for (i = 1; i <= ct; ++i)
             z *= y;                 /* Raise y to the ct power */

        return(z);

}
```

The exponential approximation used here is accurate only when its argument is more than 0 and less than 1. To compensate for this narrow range of values, a conversion process takes place at the beginning of the function. First, if the function argument, x, is a negative value (x <0), its absolute value is used. Also, if x is more than or equal to 1, its value is divided by 2 within the while loop until the result is between 0 and 1. Each time a division operation takes place, variable ct is multiplied by 2. This variable will later be used to convert to the proper exponential value.

At this point, the modified value of the function argument is passed through the exponential approximation formula. The output from this formula is then converted if necessary. If the original function argument was negative, the approximation output is divided into 1. This effectively converts the value to the negative argument equivalent. A for loop is entered and the value is modified further by raising it to the power of ct. You will remember that this variable was incremented each time the argument was divided by 2.

The result of these conversions is a value that is equivalent to the exponent of the original argument, which is returned to the calling program or function.

The accuracy of this function suffers greatly whenever the argument value is more than 10 absolute. Since this function was written especially for use with a power function, this is no great restriction, since logarithms of initial arguments to the power function will rarely exceed this value.

pwr.   At last, we have the tools to write a truly versatile power function, called pwr(). This function is terribly simple, because all of the labor has gone into building log() and exp(). The function is written as follows:

```
double pwr(x, y)    /* Return x raised to the y power */
double x, y;
{

      double log(), exp();

      return(exp(y * log(x))):

}
```

That's all there is to it. Functions log() and exp() are used in a formula discussed earlier. The pwr() function returns x to the y power. Both arguments are double types. It is now possible to raise any number to any power, provided that the numbers and result are within the processing range of your computer.

This function can be speeded up a bit by closely examining the relationships between raising a number to an integer power and raising the same number to a floating point power of slightly higher magnitude. For instance:

$$2.5 \char94 3.2$$

is the same as

$$(2.5 \char94 3) * (2.5 \char94 0.2)$$

You will notice that in the second example, a floating point value is raised to an integer power and multiplied by the product of the same value raised to a floating

point power. The sum of the integer power and the floating point power equal the
original power value in the first example. Integer math operations don't directly apply to raising a floating point value to an integer power, but this is a simple operation in C that can be handled by a for loop. This simplicity should result in increased
execution speed, as opposed to using the present version of pwr(). We can then use
pwr() to work with the floating point remainder to take 2.5 to the 0.2 power. When
the two returns are multiplied, we will have arrived at 2.5 ^ 3.2. The more efficient
version of pwr() is written in the following manner:

```
double pwr(x, y)
double x, y;
{

        double log(), exp(), d, f, yy;
        int a, c;

        d = 1;
        yy = (y < 0) ? -y : y;   /*Get abs(y) */

        if (yy > 1) {
                a = yy;     /* Get integer portion of yy */
                yy -= a;    /* Remove integer portion from yy */

                for (c = 1; c <= a; ++c)
                        d *= x;     /* Raise x to int(y) power */

                if (yy == 0)
                        return((y < 0) ? 1 / d : d);
        }

        f = exp(yy * log(x)) * d;

        return((y < 0) ? 1 / f : f);

}
```

In this function, two integer variables are used. In the first if statement line,
variable a is assigned the integer portion of the power argument, while yy is assigned only the floating point portion of this same argument.

The base argument value is taken to the integer power within the for loop.
This is borrowed directly from Kernighan and Ritchie. When the loop terminates,
variable d is equal to x raised to the power of the integer portion of the y argument.
Another if statement is used just in case the original power argument to pwr() had no
floating point portion—for example, pwr (2.1, 3.0). In such an event, the value of d
is returned, since the operation need go no further.

Assuming that there is a floating point portion, the power formula using log()

and exp() is run. Remember, this takes argument x to the power of *only* the floating point portion of y. If you assume that the original argument to pwr() was pwr (2.5, 3.2), then d = 2.5ˆ3. After exp() and log() are called, the output will be 2.5ˆ0.2. Variable f is assigned this value times d, which is the same as 2.5ˆ3.2.

Since the power argument to pwr() is always less than 1, the exp() and log() formulas work faster. The for loop portion of this program is even faster. The combined result is a more efficient pwr() function.

The final return statement includes a conversion check that modifies the return value according to whether or not a negative power argument to pwr() was passed.

TRIGONOMETRIC FUNCTIONS

Every modern language should be equipped with reliable circular functions that can calculate sines, cosines, tangents, and so on. Since many C compilers are not equipped with these UNIX math functions, this section will discuss the methods used to write them.

Fortunately, many of the tools needed to develop a large repertoire of trigonometric functions are already available in the functions that have been discussed previously. All that is really necessary is to write two new functions called sin() and cos(). These will be combined with other functions to develop a full range of trigonometric functions.

The sin Function

```
/* Return sine of arg -- arg is expressed in radians */
double sin(arg)
double arg;
{
        double a, cv, s, x;
        int m, sign;

        a = arg;
        cv = 3.1415926535897932 / 180.0;
        s = (a < 0) ? -a : a; /* Get abs(a) */

        s /= cv;        /* Convert radians to degrees */

        m = s / 360;
        s = (s >= 360) ? s - (360.0 * m) : s; /* Convert to < 360? */

        sign = (s > 90) ? -1 : 1;
        s = (s > 90) ? 180 - s : s;     /* Convert to <= 90? */
        s = (s < -90) ? 180 + s : s;    /* Convert to 1 to 89? */
        s = (s < 0) ? -s : s;           /* abs s */

        x = cv * s;     /* Convert from degrees to radians */
```

(continued)

```
        /* Calculate sine */
s = x - x * x * x / 6;
s = s + x * x * x * x * x / 120;
s = s - x * x * x * x * x * x * x / 5040;
s = s + x * x * x * x * x * x * x * x * x / 362881;
s = s - x * x * x * x * x * x * x * x * x * x * x / 39916800;
s = s + x * x * x * x * x * x * x * x * x * x * x * x * x / 6227020800
s = s + x * x * x * x * x * x * x * x * x * x * x * x * x / 6227020800

s = (arg < 0) ? -s : s;  /* Determine if arg was negative */

return(sign *s);
}
```

The sin function is based on a simple approximation that accepts an argument in radians. Although some approximations do allow for argument values expressed in degrees, radian arguments are far more common.

Although the function accepts radian arguments, as does the approximation it contains, it is still necessary to convert the initial argument to degrees. Before moving into the approximation, it is mandatory to convert back to radians. This technique is necessary because the approximation is accurate only for radian values that fall between (circularly converted) 0 and 90 degrees. Fortunately, we can easily convert from radians to degrees and then convert any degree value to an equivalency that falls within the 0 to 90 degree range required by the approximation.

At the beginning of this function, the value of the original argument (arg) is assigned to variable a. Variable cv contains the conversion formula, which is expressed as pi/180. To convert from radians to degrees, the radian value is divided by cv. To convert from degrees to radians, the degree value is multiplied by cv.

After the absolute value of a (initialized to the value of arg) is obtained, the conversion from radians to degrees takes place. The degree value of the original argument is contained in variable s. The next six function lines convert the degree value to between 0 and 90 degrees and determine whether the sine of this value will be positive or negative. For instance, the sine of 90 degrees and the sine of 270 degrees are the same, except that the first is positive and the second is negative. Therefore, if the radian value results in 270 degrees, this function converts this value to 90 degrees and assigns variable sign a value of − 1, since the sine of 270 degrees is the sine of 90 degrees multiplied by − 1. This value will be multiplied by the output from the approximation to result in a return value of the correct sign.

The degree conversion to between 0 and 90 degrees works in the following manner:

1. If radians >= 360 degrees, then convert to < 360 degrees.
2. If degrees > 90, then subtract degrees from 180.
3. If difference < − 90, then add 180.

To continue this discussion, assume that an argument of 22 (radians) is passed to this function. This will convert to 1260.50714932 degrees initially. This value will be divided by 360 degrees (m = s / 360). Since variable m has been declared an int, the fractional portion of this operation is truncated, yielding a value of 3.

The value of double variable s, is brought to within a range of 0 to 360 degrees by subtracting m * 360, or 1080. The value of s is now 180.50714932.

Variable sign will be equal to − 1, since s is more than 90 degrees. The next line subtracts the value 180.50714932 from 180, leaving the difference, − 0.50714932. Since this value is not less than − 90, the next if test proves false. Finally, variable s is assigned its absolute value of + 0.50714932. This is the value that will be passed to the sine approximation formula (after conversion back to radians) and that will yield the sine of the original argument.

Before passing the derived value to the approximation formula, it is necessary to reconvert to radians. This is done by multiplying degrees (variable s) by cv. The result is a radian value of 0.0088514255. This represents the derived value of the original argument in the same units (radians).

This value is passed through the approximation routine and the sine is output. Before making the return, several checks are made. First, the original argument is evaluated to see if it was negative. If so, the sine value from the approximation routine is multiplied by − 1. This yields the corrected sine value—so far. In the return statement, variable sign is multiplied by the value of s. The sign variable makes the final adjustment to the sine value on the basis of the conversions made while working with degrees. The return value is the sine of 22 (radians).

Accuracy is generally good to nine or ten decimal places; however, radian values that result in conversions of close to 90 degrees will not maintain this tolerance. Even in a worst-case example, accuracy is always good to six decimal places.

Some readers may wonder why I have chosen to multiply by straight mathematical representation in this and other functions. I am referring to lines such as

```
s = s + x * x * x * x * x * x * x * x;
```

Certainly, the source code would look neater if we used

```
s = s + pwr(x, 8);
```

The reason is that I am attempting to provide good precision coupled with good execution speed. The latter example calls pwr(), which, in turn, calls other functions. Since most of these functions involve approximations, any slight errors in any one function can multiply. Also, straight mathematical programming is faster than calling a function that calls other functions. The result of using this method is greatest accuracy without a sacrifice in speed.

The cos Function

Now that sin() has been written, we need another tool for a circular function building set— cos(), a function that will return the cosine of a radian value. Fortunately, the same programming methods are used for this function:

```
/* Return cosine of arg -- arg is expressed in radians */
double cos(arg)
double arg;
{
        double a, cv, s, x;
        int m, sign;

        arg = (arg < 0) ? -arg : arg;
        cv = 3.1415926535897932 / 180.0;
        s = arg;
        s /= cv;        /* Convert radians to degrees */

        m = s / 360;

        s = (s >= 360) ? s - (360.0 * m) : s; /* Convert to < 360? */
        sign = (s > 90 && s < 270) ? -1 : 1; /* Get sign */
        s = (s > 90) ? 180 - s : s;     /* Convert to <= 90? */
        s = (s < -90) ? 180 + s : s;    /* Convert to 1 to 89? */
        s = (s < 0) ? -s : s;           /* abs s */

        x = cv * s;  /* Convert degrees to radians */

                     /* Calculate cosine */
        s = 1 - x * x / 2;
        s = s + x * x * x * x / 24;
        s = s - x * x * x * x * x * x / 720;
        s = s + x * x * x * x * x * x * x * x / 40320;
        s = s - x * x * x * x * x * x * x * x * x * x / 3628800;
        s = s + x * x * x * x * x * x * x * x * x * x * x * x / 479001600;

        return(sign * s);
}
```

As before, this function converts radians to degrees and then assigns a 0 to 90 degree equivalent of the original argument. After converting back to radians, another approximation formula is used to arrive at the cosine. Further explanation can be garnered by rereading the discussion of the sin() function.

The arctan Function

To complete our set of basic trigonometric tools from which other functions can be built, a function is needed that will return the inverse tangent, or *arctangent*, of a radian value. We could also use an arcsine or arccosine function, but these are more often defined in terms of the arctangent. The following function returns the arctangent of a radian value:

```
double arctan(arg)
double arg;
{
```

```
double i, p, s, x, sqrt();
int sign;
sign = (arg < 0) ? -1 : 1;    /* Get sign of return value */
x = (arg < 0) ? -arg : arg;   /* x == abs(arg) */
x = x / sqrt(1 + x * x);
x = (x > 1) ? 1 / x : x;      /* If x > 1 use reciprocal of x */
p = 1.570796326795;      /* Pi / 2 */
i = sqrt(1 - x);

       /* Approximation routine */
s = 1.5707963050;
s = s + x * -.2145988016;
s = s + x * x * .0889789874;
s = s + x * x * x * -.0501743046;
s = s + x * x * x * x *.0308918810;
s = s + x * x * x * x * x * -.0170881256;
s = s + x * x * x * x * x * x * .0066700901;
s = s + x * x * x * x * x * x * x * - .0012624911;
s = p - i * s;
s = (arg > 1 || arg < -1) ? p - s : s;

return(s * sign);

}
```

The argument must be passed to the approximation routine as a value equal to or greater than 0 and less than or equal to 1. Negative arguments are converted to absolute value at the beginning of the function. If the abs value is more than 1, the reciprocal is used. A later function line tests for a value of 1 and subtracts the approximation output value from pi/2.

Building Other Functions

With the bevy of functions already discussed, it is now quite easy to build the remaining functions needed to complete a set. Tangents, cotangents, secants, cosecants, and so forth, are simply derivatives of sine, cosine, arctan, and other functions that have been discussed.

The tan function.   The tangent function, tan(), is based on the formula

$$tangent\ (x)\ =\ sine(x)\ /\ cosine(x)$$

When we know how to get the sine and cosine of a value, deriving the tangent is a matter of simple mathematics. The following function returns the tangent of a radian value:

```
double tan(x)
double x;
{
```

(*continued*)

```
    double sin(), cos(), s, c;

    s = sin(x);
    c = cos(x);

    return((s == 0 || c == 0) ? 1000 : s / c);

}
```

This function first gets the sine and cosine of the argument through calls to sin() and cos(). The return values are divided, and the tangent of the argument is passed back to the calling program. If either sin(x) or cos(x) is equal to 0, this represents infinity. In this function, the value 1000 is returned for infinity. This is an arbitrary value that can be altered to suit individual preferences.

The cot function.   A function to return the contangent of a radian value is a simple reverse of the tangent function. This new function, cot(), is based on the simple formula

cotangent = cosine / sine

The cotangent function is written as follows:

```
double cot(x)
double x;
{

    double sin(), cos() , s, c;

    s = sin(x);
    c = cos(x);

    return((s == 0 || c == 0) ? 1000 : c / s);

}
```

The only difference between tan() and cot() is the divide operation within the return statement line. Again, the arbitrary value of 1000 is returned to represent infinity.

The sec function.   The secant of a radian value is the reciprocal of its cosine, or

secant = 1 / cosine

The function sec() returns the secant of its argument:

```
double sec(x)
double x;
{

    double cos(), c;

    c = cos(x);

    return((c == 0) ? 1000 : 1 / c);

}
```

This function will execute a bit faster than tan() or cot() because it calls only cos(), rather than both sin() and cos().

The csec function.   The cosecant of a value is the reciprocal of its sine. The csec() function returns the cosecant, as follows:

```
double csec(x)
double x;
{

    double sin(), s;

    s = sin(x);

    return((s == 0) ? 1000 : 1 / s);

}
```

This function completes the standard list of trigonometric functions. By writing sin() and cos(), we had all of the tools to build the remaining functions at hand.

INVERSE TRIGONOMETRIC FUNCTIONS

The following functions depend mainly on arctan() to return the inverse sine, cosine, cotangent, secant, and cosecant of a radian value.

Inverse Sine

```
double arcsin(x)
double x;
{

     double arctan(), sqrt();

     return(arctan(x / sqrt(1 - x * x)));

}
```

Inverse Cosine

```
double arccos(x)
double x;
{

     double arctan(), sqrt();

     return(1.570796326 - arctan(x / sqrt(1 - x
     * x)));

}
```

Inverse Cotangent

```
double arccot(x)
double x;
{

     double arctan();

     return(1.570796326 - arctan(x));

}
```

Inverse Secant

```
double arcsec(x)
double x;
{

     double arccos();

     return(arccos(1 / x));

}
```

Inverse Cosecant

```
double arccsc(x)
double x;
{

        double arcsin();

        return(arcsin(1 / x));

}
```

HYPERBOLIC FUNCTIONS

The following functions return the hyperbolic sine, cosine, tangent, cotangent, secant, and cosecant of a value. They are presented without discussion, because each
calls a function that has already been presented.

Hyperbolic Sine

```
double sinh(x)
double x;
{

        double exp();

        return((exp(x) - exp(-x)) / 2);

}
```

Hyperbolic Cosine

```
double cosh(x)
double x;
{
double exp();

        return((exp(x) + exp(-x)) / 2);

}
```

Hyperbolic Tangent

```
double tanh(x)
double x;
}

        double exp();

        return((exp(x) - exp(-x)) / (exp(x) -
        (exp(-x))));

}
```

Hyperbolic Cotangent

```
double coth(x)
double x;
{

        double exp();

        return((exp(x) + exp(-x)) / (exp(x) -
        exp(-x)));

}
```

Inverse Hyperbolic Sine

```
double arcsinh(x)
double x;
{

        double log(), sqrt();

        return(log(x + sqrt(x * x + 1)));

}
```

Inverse Hyperbolic Cosine

```
double arccosh(x)
double x;
{

        double log(), sqrt();

        return(log(x + sqrt(x * x -1)));

}
```

Inverse Hyperbolic Tangent

```
double arctanh(x)
double x;
{

        double log();

        return(log((1 + x) / (1 - x)) / 2);

}
```

Inverse Hyperbolic Cotangent

```
  double arccoth(x)
  double x;
  {

        double log();

        return(log((x + 1) / (x - 1)) / 2);

  }
```

Inverse Hyperbolic Secant

```
        double arcsech(x)
        double x;
        {

                double arccosh();

                return(arcosh(1 / x));

        }
```

Inverse Hyperbolic Cosecant

```
        double arccsch(x)
        double x;
        }

                double arcsinh();

                return(1 / arcsinh(x));

        }
```

HOW GOOD ARE THESE FUNCTIONS?

The question that heads this section is an appropriate one, but its answer will depend on many different factors. If your present C compiler is not equipped with these functions, they are obviously better than nothing at all. If your compiler does include all or most of the functions discussed in this chapter, the answer will depend on the quality of the compiler's math function library.

This section will compare many of the functions discussed in this chapter with those found as part of the Lattice C compiler. The latest version as of this writing, Version 2.14, does include many of the UNIX math functions. The following tests were performed using the Lattice compiler running under MS-DOS 2.1. The test machine is the IBM Personal Computer, with 640K RAM and the 8087 math coprocessor. It should be remembered that the coprocessor greatly speeds up the execution time of programs and functions that utilize floating point arithmetic. If your computer is not equipped with the 8087, execution speed will be slower, but accuracy should be consistent with the figures printed in these pages. For serious applications that depend greatly on execution speed, I believe that a math coprocessor is mandatory for the IBM Personal Computer and other similar MS-DOS compatible machines that use the 8088 microprocessor operating at 4.77 MHz. By today's standards, such machines are quite slow, especially when compared with computers using the 8086 microprocessor at 7 to 8 MHz. Those machines execute much faster, and a math coprocessor may not be as necessary.

Before beginning the discussion on the results of benchmark tests, a few generalizations are in order. The following tests should indicate that the functions discussed in this chapter are significantly faster than those found in the compiler's math library. However, this speed increase is generally gained through a sacrifice in accuracy. My functions are generally accurate to at least seven decimal places, whereas the compiler's functions exhibit accuracy from nine to twelve decimal places.

It would be possible to increase the accuracy of personally written functions to this degree; but this may not be a practical trade-off, as execution speed might be reduced by a factor of three. I think you will discover that for all but the most demanding scientific applications, the functions in this text will serve quite well. They will excel if you don't require more than single-precision accuracy, as many of them execute three times faster than those in the Lattice compiler.

The following tests are presented to give the reader a general idea of the performance of my functions compared with those in the compiler's math library. These are very simple benchmark tests that will indicate the time required to access a function a certain number of times. The speeds will be compared, and the output values of each function will be compared for accuracy. This should provide the reader with a fair evaluation.

The programs used to test the various functions have the following general format:

```
main()
{

    double fctn(), x, y;

    for (x = start; x <= end; (++)inc)
        y = fctn((double) x);

}



/* fctn() = function being tested */
/* start = starting value */
/* end = ending value */
/* (++)inc = incrementing value */
```

This program simply makes calls (usually 1000) to fctn(), using the for loop to increment the value of x in steps of (+ +)inc. Even though this is an integer step and integer values are actually used, they are represented in floating point format to satisfy the function requirement of being passed a floating point value.

Results

	Lattice	Traister
Function	sqrt()	sqrt ()
Start:end	1:1000	1:1000
Time (seconds)	46	14
Accuracy (D places)	14	14

Comments: My function seems to be superior to the commercial version tested. It is more than three times faster and exhibits the same accuracy.

	Lattice	Traister
Function	NA	cubrt()
Start:end	NA	1:1000
Time (seconds)	NA	17
Accuracy (D places)	NA	13

Comments: Although this function is not included as part of the commercial library used for comparison, it is a part of the UNIX math library. Its speed and accuracy are of commercial quality.

	Lattice	Traister
Function	NA	root ()
Start:end	NA	1:1000
Time (seconds)	NA	20
Accuracy (D places)	NA	13

Comments: Although this function is not a standard part of any math library, it is quite useful for taking integer roots of numbers. It is very fast and accurate.

	Lattice	Traister
Function	log ()	log ()
Start:end	1:1000	1:1000
Time (seconds)	25	20
Accuracy (D places)	12	More than 7

Comments: This function was a bit of a disappointment. It is not appreciably faster than the commercial version and does not match its accuracy. For applications in which the lower precision is no problem, the slight speed increase may be an advantage.

	Lattice	Traister
Function	exp ()	exp()
Start:end	.001:1.00	.001:1.00
Time (seconds)	16	8
Accuracy (D places)	12	9

Comments: My exp function compared favorably with the commercial version. It is twice as fast and generally accurate to nine decimal places. It is limited in range, however. Values greater than abs (10) will severely affect accuracy. The commercial version does not suffer from this problem. In most applications, the range limitation should pose no problem.

	Lattice	Traister
Function	pow ()	pwr ()
Start:end	.1:100	.1:100
Time (seconds)	44	32
Accuracy (D places)	10–12	6–11

Comments: Since both functions depend on the quality of log() and exp(), in terms of both speed and precision, these results are not unexpected. My function is considerably faster than the commercial version, but its accuracy fluctuates over a wider range.

	Lattice	Traister
Function	sin ()	sin ()
Start:end	.001:1.00	.001:1.00
Time (seconds)	35	8
Accuracy (D places)	10–14	8–14

Comments: My sin function is quite good. It is nearly five times faster than the commercial version, and it exhibits comparable accuracy. However, accuracy will suffer when arguments close to 90 degrees are passed to this function, dropping to eight decimal places.

	Lattice	Traister
Function	cos ()	cos ()
Start:end	.001:1.00	.001:1.00
Time (seconds)	35	8
Accuracy (D places)	10–14	8–14

Comments: See sin () function comments.

	Lattice	Traister
Function	atan ()	arctan ()
Start:end	.001:1.00	.001:1.00
Time (seconds)	117	24
Accuracy (D places)	10	8

Comments: My arctan function compares quite favorably to the commercial version. It is nearly five times faster, and it is accurate to eight decimal places, compared with ten decimal places for atan ().

In fairness to the reader, it should be explained that these are general comparisons carried out with a stopwatch; they were not made in accordance with strict scientific rules for conducting true benchmark testing. Precision was determined from a few arguments of different value ranges. A more structured test of the various function attributes would have searched for anomalies or instances in which unusual accuracy or inaccuracy might exist.

Many of the functions presented and discussed to this point do not match the commercial functions in precision. However, they make up for this lack with greatly accelerated execution speed in most cases. These functions will greatly enhance compilers that do not contain a set of UNIX math functions. For compilers that do, the alternate functions presented here will complement the present math library and may be used where speed of execution is more important than twelve-place precision.

GREATER SPEED

A large number of math functions have been presented that offer a pleasing compromise between execution speed and accuracy. Although all of them were considerably faster than the commercial versions with which they were compared, more speed may be needed, especially for graphics applications in which thousands or hundreds of thousands of pixels must be set on a screen according to a geometric equation. Such equations typically make calls to sin() and cos() and possibly to sqrt(), tan(), exp(), and so forth.

There are several ways to increase execution speed: writing more efficient code, buying a faster microcomputer, or installing a special high-speed processor board in your present computer. The last two methods are usually not practical for most microcomputer owners. One hardware method is practical, however. If your computer is not equipped with a math coprocessor, and it is designed to accept one, this relatively inexpensive addition can do much to speed up your C language functions. This assumes, of course, that your C compiler will support such a device. The 8087 math coprocessor for the IBM PC and compatables can mean the difference between sluggish, inefficient programs and entirely satisfactory programs.

Still, there must be other avenues to try in terms of more efficient code. This chapter is devoted to this end. In the preceding section, execution speed was a prime requisite, but so was accuracy. Although some accuracy was sacrificed for speed, some speed was sacrificed for accuracy as well. Though some programmers may argue with me, the previously discussed functions are about as efficient as they can be, assuming that the same approximations are to be used. Certainly, since each function was written in a form that would offer the reader the best possibility of comprehension, a line or two of code might be enhanced for a minimal increase in speed. However, I don't think any drastic speed increases can be garnered from these functions.

The only alternative is to sacrifice accuracy for speed. This is accomplished by using other approximations that are mathematically less complex. Less complexity should result directly in a faster algorithm. However, the accuracy will be degraded—in some cases, drastically.

In a graphics environment, function accuracy to eight or nine decimal places is not a major requirement. After all, pixels are ultimately set on the graphics screen through a system of integer coordinates. If a pixel coordinate is to be specified by [sqrt(2), sqrt(8.6)] for the *x*, *y* axis, then the actual coordinates for this pixel will be (1, 3), the integer equivalents of the sqrt() output. For such uses, a function that returns a square root need only be accurate to one decimal place, and in many instances, the integer equivalent of the square root is all that is required.

The square root function discussed previously was very efficient in all ways. It offered twelve-place accuracy and excellent execution speed. You will recall that this speed was a product of an integer square root routine that returned an approximation to a floating point square root routine. If all you require is the integer square root of a floating point value, then all that is necessary is to delete the floating point algorithm from sqrt(), and have the function return what was originally the integer approximation. This will make an already fast function much faster—but at the sacrifice of accuracy.

In this usage, the accuracy sacrifice is of no consequence, and this will be the case in many programming environments. The reader who needs extremely fast C functions and who requires accuracies of no greater than two or three decimal places will be pleased to know that many approximations are available to allow for these requirements.

The sine Function

Although the previously discussed sin() function is very fast, it simply will not be adequate for serious forays into C language graphics. A sine function is normally used when dealing with the production of circles, arcs, and other shapes on the graphics screen. A faster function is needed to meet graphic requirements. The following one offers greatly increased speed:

```
/* 4 seconds for 1000 calls; accuracy 3-5 decimal places */
/* Return sine of arg -- arg is expressed in radians */
double sine(arg)
double arg;
{

    double a, cv, s, x;
    int m, sign;

    a = arg;
    cv = 3.1415926535897932 / 180.0;

    s = (a < 0) ? -a : a; /* Get abs(a) */

    s /= cv;        /* Convert radians to degrees */
```

(continued)

```
m = s / 360;
s = (s >= 360) ? s - (360.0 * m) : s; /* Convert to < 360? */
sign = (s > 90) ? -1 : 1;
s = (s > 90) ? 180 - s : s;      /* Convert to <= 90? */
s = (s < -90) ? 180 + s : s;     /* Convert to 1 to 89? */
s = (s < 0) ? -s : s;            /* abs s */

x = cv * s;      /* Convert from degrees to radians */

        /* Calculate sine */
s = 1 + -.16605 * x * x;
s = s + .00761 * x * x * x * x;

s = (arg < 0) ? -s : s;  /* Determine if arg was negative */

return(sign * s * x);
```

```
}
```

This is the same function discussed earlier, except that the approximation routine has been shortened. This one only requires taking the modified value of the argument to powers of 2 and 4, respectively. Since the approximation is shorter and less complex, the function executes much faster. This one required only 4 seconds for 1000 calls. This is twice as fast as the previous version, which, in turn, was nearly five times faster than the commercial version tested. Still greater speed can be obtained with further modifications.

This function accepts a radian argument, which is then converted to degrees. Another conversion routine pulls the degree value to within a range of 0 to 90 degrees. Obviously, these conversions take time. They are necessary because the approximation formula is accurate only when handling radian values of between 0 and pi/2, the equivalent of 0 to 90 degrees.

A sine function is often a part of graphics routines used for plotting circles. However, not every point on the circumference is plotted. In fact, it is only necessary to plot the points for one quarter-circle. When these are known, mirror-image arcs can be quickly plotted through integer mathematics. Therefore, to draw a perfect circle, all that is needed in a sine function is the capability to plot sines of integer values over a range of 0 to 90 degrees. This is exactly what the following function is designed to do:

```
/* Return sine of arg -- arg is expressed as 0 - 90 degrees */
double sin(arg)
int arg;
{
    double cv, s, x;

    cv = 3.1415926535897932 / 180.0;
    s = arg;
    x = cv * s;      /* Convert from degrees to radians */
```

```
           /* Calculate sine */
   s = 1 + -.16605 * x * x;
   s = s + .00761 * x * x * x * x * x;

   return(s * x);

}
```

This might be called a "dedicated" function, in that it was written specifically for calculating the y-axis coordinates for a quarter-circle, based on an *integer* input of from 0 to 90 degrees. It illustrates how functions can be custom-tailored to address specific applications, with the programmer determining what is necessary in both precision and execution speed.

The cos Function

A function that returns the cosine of a value is also quite necessary in graphics endeavors. The sine function cannot plot the coordinates of a quarter-circle by itself. It is used in conjunction with cos() to plot the x, y arc axis using the following formula:

$$x = \text{radius} * \cos(\text{degree}) + a$$

$$y = \text{radius} * \sin(\text{degree}) + b$$

where *a* and *b* name the center of the circle.

This function returns the cosine of a radian value:

```
/* 4 seconds  for 1000  calls ; accurate 3-5 decimal places */
/* Return cosine of arg -- arg is expressed in radians */
double cos(arg)
double arg;

{

    double a, cv, s, x;
    int m, sign;

    arg = (arg < 0) ? -arg : arg;
    cv = 3.1415926535897932 / 180.0;
    s = arg;
    s /= cv;        /* Convert radians to degrees */

    m = s / 360;

    s = (s >= 360) ? s - (360.0 * m) : s; /* Convert to < 360? */
    sign = (s > 90 && s < 270) ? -1 : 1; /* Get sign */
    s = (s > 90) ? 180 - s : s;    /* Convert to <= 90? */
    s = (s < -90) ? 180 + s : s;   /* Convert to 1 to 89? */
    s = (s < 0) ? -s : s;          /* abs s */
```

(continued)

```
      x = cv * s;   /* Convert degrees to radians */

                    /* Calculate cosine */
      s = 1 + -.49670 * x * x;
      s = s + .03705 * x * x * x * x;

      return(sign * s);

}
```

This is the previous cosine function with its long approximation routine replaced by a far shorter one. This one is twice as fast as the previous version, with three- to five-place accuracy. It will accept any radian value, which is then converted to 0 to pi/2 before being passed on to the approximation routine.

To convert this function to accept an argument of 0 to 90 degrees, the same steps are taken as with the sine function just discussed. The resulting function is

```
/* Return cosine of arg -- arg is expressed as 0 - 90 degrees */
double cos(arg)
int arg;
{

      double cv, s, x;

      cv = 3.1415926535897932 / 180.0;
      s = arg;
      x = cv * s;   /* Convert degrees to radians */

                    /* Calculate cosine */
      s = 1 + -.49670 * x * x;
      s = s + .03705 * x * x * x * x;

      return(s);

}
```

This function and the last version of sin() require about 2 seconds for 1000 calls. Therefore, for dedicated purposes, it can be said that they are four times faster than the equivalents discussed earlier or nearly twenty times faster than the commercial versions. Their accuracy is not great, but it is more than adequate for the dedicated purpose.

The following function draws a circle on the graphics screen using sin() and cos():

```
/* setpix() places a pixel at the coordinates specified */
circle(a, b, r)
int a, b, r;
{
int n, i, j, k, m, n, t, x, y;
double sin(), cos();
```

```
h = a + r;
i = a - r;
j = b + r;
k = b - r;

for (t = 0; t <= 90; ++t) {
    x = r * cos(t) + a;
    y = r * sin(t) + b;
    setpix(x, y);        /* First arc */
    m = k + (j - y);
    setpix(x, m);        /* Second arc */
    n = i + (h - x);
    setpix(n, y);        /* Third arc */
    setpix(n, m);        /* Fourth arc */
}
```

In this function, setpix() is simply representative of any function that allows a pixel to be set on the graphics screen on the basis of the *x*, *y* coordinates that serve as its arguments. This function is not usable until setpix() is replaced with the proper function call provided by any graphics library the reader may be using. You might also try this program using the earlier versions of sin() and cos() or, if available, a commercial version of these functions. The speed differences will be quite apparent.

These comparisons will help define just what is meant by a "quality" mathematical function. Such a definition will depend on the uses of the function. A quality function for scientific purposes might exhibit excellent precision, but it would undoubtedly be a poor function for graphics environments because of its slow speed. On the other hand, a quality graphics function might rightly be classified as a poor scientific function because of its low precision.

To be completely accurate and fair, it should be stressed that many of the best graphics functions depend little on complex mathematical formulas. The highest speeds are obtained by using look-up tables that contain all of the necessary values. In the preceding function, sin() and cos() are called 91 times, each time the circle function is executed, and they always return the same sequence. An even faster function would eliminate these calls completely and replace them with the values they return during the integer count from 0 to 90. The function would then appear as follows:

```
circle(a, b, r)
int a, b, r;
{

    int h, i, j, k, m, n,t, x, y;
```

(continued)

```
static double sincos[91][2] = {
        { 1 ,   0 },
        { .9998478 ,   1.745239E-02 },
        { .9993909 ,   3.489947E-02 },
        { .9986296 ,   5.233592E-02 },
        { .9975641 ,   6.975641E-02 },
        { .9961948 ,   8.715567E-02 },
        { .927184 ,   .3746063 },
        { .920505 ,   .3907308 },
        { .9135456 ,   .4067364 },
        { .906308 ,   .4226179 },
        { .8987942 ,   .4383708 },
        { .8910067 ,   .4539902 },
        { .8829477 ,   .4694712 },
        { .8746199 ,   .4848093 },
        { .8660257 ,   .4999997 },
        { .8571676 ,   .5150377 },
        { .8480483 ,   .5299189 },
        { .8386709 ,   .5446386 },
        { .8290378 ,   .5591925 },
        { .8191524 ,   .573576 },
        { .8090175 ,   .5877849 },
        { .7986358 ,   .6018146 },
        { .7880111 ,   .615661 },
        { .7771461 ,   .62932 },
        { .7660448 ,   .6427871 },
        { .75471 ,   .6560586 },
        { .7431453 ,   .6691301 },
        { .7313541 ,   .6819979 },
        { .7193402 ,   .694658 },
        { .7071073 ,   .7071063 },
        { .6946588 ,   .7193394 },
        { .6819989 ,   .7313533 },
        { .6691313 ,   .7431444 },
        { .6560595 ,   .7547091 },
        { .6427882 ,   .766044 },
        { .629321 ,   .7771455 },
        { .615662 ,   .7880103 },
        { .6018156 ,   .798635 },
        { .587786 ,   .8090166 },
        { .5735771 ,   .8191516 },
        { .5591935 ,   .8290371 },
        { .5446397 ,   .8386701 },
        { .52992 ,   .8480478 },
```

```
{ .5150389 ,    .8571669 },
{ .5000009 ,    .866025 },
{ .4848102 ,    .8746192 },
{ .4694722 ,    .8829472 },
{ .4539913 ,    .8910061 },
{ .4383721 ,    .8987936 },
{ .4226192 ,    .9063074 },
{ .4067377 ,    .9135451 },
{ .3907321 ,    .9205044 },
{ .3746074 ,    .9271835 },
{ .3583689 ,    .9335801 },
{ .3420212 ,    .9396922 },
{ .3255692 ,    .9455183 },
{ .3090178 ,    .9510563 },
{ .2923728 ,    .9563045 },
{ .2756383 ,    .9612614 },
{ .2588201 ,    .9659256 },
{ .2419231 ,    .9702956 },
{ .2249522 ,    .9743698 },
{ .2079126 ,    .9781474 },
{ .1908099 ,    .9816271 },
{ .1736492 ,    .9848076 },
{ .1564356 ,    .9876881 },
{ .1391744 ,    .990268 },
{ .1218708 ,    .992546 },
{ .1045297 ,    .9945219 },
{ 8.715691E-02 ,    .9961946 },
{ .0697576 ,    .9975639 },
{ 5.233722E-02 ,    .9986295 },
{ .0349009 ,    .9993908 },
{ 1.745395E-02 ,    .9998477 },
{ 1.310775E-06 ,    1 }

};

h = a + r;
i = a - r;
j = b + r;
k = b - r;
```

(continued)

```
for (t = 0; t <= 90; ++t) {
    x = r * sincos[t][0] + a;
    y = r * sincos[t][1] + b;
    pixset(x, y);
    m = k + (j - y);
    pixset(x, m);
    n = i + (h - x);
    pixset(n, y);
    pixset(n, m);
}

}
```

Obviously, writing such a function can involve much more keyboard time, but the access time for 1000 calls is a fraction of a second because no complex mathematical operations take place. There are no approximations here. The cosines and sines of values 0 to 90 degrees are contained within the array. Simple mathematics is performed to draw versions of the arc whose coordinates are obtained from the array items. The combination of these four arcs forms a circle.

This function is used just like the previous one. Its arguments consist of the coordinates of the circle center (a, b) and the circle radius (r). Knowing these values and having the capability of drawing the 0 to 90 degree arc are all that is needed to produce the three remaining arcs. The speed with which a circle will be produced is then more a factor of the efficiency of the graphics function, generically called pixset. Typically, this function will work more slowly than the access time required to retrieve the cosine/sine information.

This version of circle() involves programming a look-up table into the function for highest possible speed. A later section of this chapter will discuss this mode of function programming in more detail and will show methods whereby look-up tables of a thousand items and more can be produced in a few minutes.

The arctan Function

As is the case with most mathematical functions, there are ways to speed up arctan() at the cost of precision. The following function quickly returns the arctangent of a radian value:

```
/* 2 seconds for 1000 calls; accurate to 3-4 decimal places */
double arctan(x)
double x;
{
    double s, t;

    s = (x > 1 || x < -1) ? 1 / x : x;
    s = s / (1 + .28 * s * s);
```

```
     return((x > 1 || x < -1) ? 1.57079 - s : s);
}
```

This function accepts any radian value, although the approximation is set up to accept values between − 1 and 1. As with previous functions, when a value exceeds this range, its reciprocal is used. The output from the approximation is subtracted from the value of pi/2 if the reciprocal was used before making the return. If not, the output from the approximation, unaltered, is returned.

This function is quick, requiring only 2 seconds for 1000 calls. This is a major speed improvement compared to the more accurate version in the previous section, which took 8 seconds for the same amount of calls. The commercial version in the Lattice compiler took 117 seconds.

The log Function

Just as there is often a need for fast circular functions, certain programming situations require the same execution efficiency for log(). This version is very quick and accurate to about four decimal places:

```
/* access time 6 seconds for 1000 calls. Accurate to 4 dp */
double log(x)       /*Return natural logarithm of x */
double x;
{
     int ct, lt;
     double t, y;

     ct = lt = 0;

     while (x < 1) {
          x *= 10;
          ++lt;
     }

     while (x > 2.0) {
          x /= 2.0;
          ++ct;
     }

/* Derive log(x) through polynomial approximation */

     t = x - 1;
     y = .99949556 * t;
     y = y + -.49190896 * t * t;
     y = y + .28947478 * t * t * t;
     y = y + -.13606275 * t * t * t * t;
     y = y + .03215845 * t * t * t * t * t;

     return(y + (ct * 0.6931471805599453) - (lt * 2.3025850929940457));
}
```

The 6 seconds required for 1000 calls is more than three times faster than the log function discussed earlier. It could be made even faster if the argument could be held within a range of 1 to 2. The four-place accuracy isn't too bad, so this function could be readily used with the exp() function that follows to arrive at a quick pwr() function that is accurate to two or three decimal places.

The exp Function

This function will complete the tool kit of "fast" functions from which other fast functions can be built. Methods for combining the functions presented here to arrive at others can be found in an earlier section.

The fast exp() function is written as follows:

```
/* 2 seconds for 1000 calls; accurate to 2-3 decimal places */
double exp(b)
double b;
{
        int ct, i;
        double x, y, z;

        x = (b < 0) ? -b : b;   /* Get abs b */
        ct = y = z = 1;

        while (x >= 1) {
                x /= 2;   /* Divide x by 2 */
                ct *= 2; /* Return multiplier */
        }

/* Exponential approximation */

        y += -.9664 * x;
        y += .3536 * x * x;

        y = (b < 0) ? y : 1 / y;   /* Determine final value */

        for (i = 1; i <= ct; ++i)
                z *= y;                 /* Raise y to the ct power */

        return(z);

}
```

This is a copy of the previous exp() function, but its complex approximation routine has been replaced with a far simpler one. It can be made more efficient by eliminating the conversion routines at the opening. This assumes that the argument values will be kept between 0 and 1. The 2 seconds required for 1000 calls is excellent, but the accuracy is good only to two decimal places dependably.

By combining the functions discussed in this section on speedy functions, it is possible to match all those presented in the previous section. The execution speed of these fast functions will rival that of the others, but this speed has cost a great deal in precision. Still, precision is not the main concern in many applications for which speed is crucial. In any event, the functions presented in these sections should make an excellent addition to any compiler library. The extra versatility available from such a library can mean far more efficient C programs. After all, it would be foolish to use a slow function with excellent precision when a very fast function with low precision would serve as well or probably better. On the other hand, you should not be forced into using a fast function when speed is not important but precision is. With a complete set of functions (slow, fast, and very fast), a great deal of versatility is built into your compiler library. Now you can enter many different programming areas with a full and proper tool kit of C functions.

GREATER ACCURACY

If you need greater accuracy from math functions, it will be necessary to use approximations that are usually far more complex than those that have been discussed to this point. This will mean slower execution times, of course, but where accuracy is important, speed may not be essential.

For most microcomputer environments, the functions presented so far should be accurate enough for the great majority of applications. Recall, however, that the first log() function presented was a bit of a disappointment. It was moderately fast, but its accuracy was not particularly good. Since log() may be used to build many other functions, I decided to try a longer and slower route toward accuracy.

It is difficult to be involved in computer mathematical functions for very long without coming in contact with something called a *Chebyshev polynomial* or *Chebyshev approximation*. This is a long polynomial series that can yield very accurate results if carried through enough steps. Each step involves raising an argument to many different powers, so this method is bound to be slow in comparison to some of the other approximations discussed earlier.

Although I suspect that many C functions contained in commercial software adjuncts for C compilers use Chebyshev approximations, I have shied away from them for most of the functions in this text. There are many other approximations that are almost as good and exhibit far better execution speed. Also, a text filled with functions that use Chebyshev approximations would be quite difficult for most readers. The source code for most of these functions would be strung out over several pages, and because of the need to continuously raise arguments to many powers, reader comprehension might suffer by volume alone.

The log Function

The log function will illustrate the complexity of a Chebyshev approximation. Admittedly, most of this complexity can be attributed to the ''appearance'' of the source code, which could be cleaned up a bit by using a function like pow() or pwr() to take an argument to various powers. The long strings of straight arithmetic multiplication would be eliminated, but speed would suffer because of these added function calls. To make this function a bit more comprehensible, I have chosen to make each of the steps in the approximation a separate function, called tzero(), tone(), ttwo(), and so on. Each of these steps passes the argument through a stage of the polynomial. The return value is then multiplied by another portion of the approximation. The end result will be the logarithm of the original argument, accurate to from eight to eleven decimal places. This particular approximation actually returns log(1 + arg), so the value of the original argument is modified before it is passed to the Chebyshev formula. Regardless of what the original value is, it will be transformed to within a range of 1 to 2. The output from the approximation is altered within the return statement line to reflect these changes, so the final return value is the logarithm of the original argument. The function is written as follows:

```
double log(x)      /*Return natural logarithm of x */
double x;
{
      int ct, lt;
      double  a,  tzero(),   tone(),   ttwo(),   tthree(),    tfour(),
tfive(), tsix(), tseven(), teight(), tnine(), tten(), televen();

      ct = lt = 0;

      while (x < 1) {
            x *= 10;
            ++lt;
      }

      while (x > 2.0) {
            x /= 2.0;
            ++ct;
      }

/* Derive log(x) through Chebyshev Polynomial */

      x -= 1;
      x = 2 * x - 1;

      a = 0.376452813;
      a = a + tone(x) * 0.343145750;
      a = a + ttwo(x) * -0.029437252;
      a = a + tthree(x) * 0.003367089;
      a = a + tfour(x) * -0.000433276;
      a = a + tfive(x) * 0.000059471;
      a = a + tsix(x) * -0.000008503;
      a = a + tseven(x) * 0.000001250;
      a = a + teight(x) * -0.000000188;
      a = a + tnine(x) * 0.000000029;
```

```
        a = a + tten(x) * -0.000000004;
        a = a + televen(x) * .000000001;

        return(a + (ct * 0.6931471805599453) - (lt * 2.3025850929940457));

}

double tzero(x)
double x;
{

        return(1.0);

}
double tone(x)
double x;
{

        return(x);

}
double ttwo(x)
double x;
{

        return(2 * x * x - 1);

}
double tthree(x)
double x;
{

        return(4 * x * x * x - 3 * x);

}
double tfour(x)
double x;
{

        return(8 * x * x * x * x  - 8 * x * x + 1);

}
double tfive(x)
double x;
{

        return(16 * x * x * x * x * x - 20 * x * x * x + 5 * x);

}

double tsix(x)
double x;
{

        return(32 * x * x * x * x * x  * x - 48 * x * x * x * x + 18 *

x * x - 1);

}
```

(*continued*)

```
double tseven(x)
double x;
{

      return(64 * x * x * x * x * x * x * x - 112 * x * x * x * x *
x + 56 * x * x * x - 7 * x);

}
double teight(x)
double x;
{

      return(128 * x *  x * x * x * x * x * x * x - 256 * x * x * x
* x * x * x + 160 * x * x * x * x - 32 * x * x + 1);

}
double tnine(x)
double x;
{

      return(256 * x * x * x * x * x *  x * x * x * x - 576 * x * x
* x * x * x * x * x + 432 * x * x * x * x * x * x -120 * x * x * x + x
* x);

}
double tten(x)
double x;
{

      return(512 * x * x * x * x * x * x * x * x * x * x -1280 *  x
* x * x * x * x * x * x * x + 1120 * x * x * x * x * x * x * x - 400 *
x * x * x * x + 50 * x * x -1);

}
double televen(x)
double x;
{

      return(1024 * x  * x * x *  x * x * x  * x * x * x * x -
2816 * x * x * x * x * x * x * x * x * x + 2816  * x * x * x * x *
x * x * x - 1232 * x * x * x * x * x + 220 * x * x * x - 11 * x);

}
```

As you can see, this function requires long study rather than a quick glance. The Chebyshev polynomial is contained in functions tzero() through televen(). The approximation proper is the set of values by which the return value from each Chebyshev function is multiplied. An approximation for another function, such as exp(), can use the same Chebyshev functions shown here. They remain a constant series. Only the approximation portion will change—that is, the multipliers for the return values from tzero() through televen(). Therefore, the Chebyshev functions used here may be applied to any other approximation function that uses the Chebyshev polynomial.

Incidentally, there are several different Chebyshev polynomials. The one used in this function is called the "Chebyshev polynomial of the first kind." Fortunately, the other polynomials are derivatives of this one, so these functions should be useful regardless of which polynomial version is called for.

Be aware that a Chebyshev approximation is really an approximation based on multiplying values worked through the Chebyshev formulas by specially derived values. Therefore, a Chebyshev approximation can be very accurate or very inaccurate, depending on its quality. The log() function shown here is based on twelve Chebyshev steps—tzero() through televen(). Approximations that use fewer steps will be less precise.

As previously stated, this log() function is far more accurate than versions discussed earlier in this text. Precision depends on input value, but even in severe cases, accuracy was maintained to a least eight decimal places and usually to nine or more. Execution speed is slow, requiring about 38 seconds for 1000 calls. However, the version shown here is not as efficient as it could be because of the programming of each Chebyshev step as a separate function. This was done to make the function more comprehensible. If the contents of each function were placed within the body of the calling function, execution speed would be increased. More accuracy could be obtained by altering the approximation to use even more Chebyshev steps, but the law of diminishing returns would quickly take hold and significant improvements would become harder to obtain.

A search through any good math text will reveal many approximations based on the Chebyshev polynomials. By using the Chebyshev functions contained in log(), it should be possible to quickly arrive at a function based on these approximations.

There are many other approximations for every mathematical function discussed in this text. Some of them offer great accuracy; others are less accurate but have great speed when used in computer programs. This book uses some of each type and many that form a compromise between speed and accuracy. The greater accuracy that has been touched on in this section comes with a great sacrifice in execution speed, and it might seem that there is no way to achieve maximum speed and maximum precision in the same program. This is not totally correct. The next section will take some of what has been learned to this point and present a method by which a C function may be extremely fast *and* extremely accurate.

EXCEPTIONAL SPEED AND ACCURACY

As the title of this section implies, it is possible to write functions that contain the near ultimate in speed and accuracy to many decimal places. How is this accomplished? The task does not seem easy. Obviously, the precision of any function can be increased by means of a more complex approximation formula, but this will also lead to increased execution time. The opposite is also true. The execution time can be increased by resorting to simpler approximations, but then the precision suffers terribly.

The answer was hinted at in an earlier section where a look-up table was used to replace sin() and cos(). Each and every cosine and sine of a range of numbers between 0 and 90 was placed in an array that was accessed by a simple bit of integer arithmetic to determine which value was sought, on the basis of the input argument value. This form of writing C functions can be applied to every other function previously discussed.

"This is simply not practical!" is the usual response when look-up tables are suggested, but as with all types of programming, there are right ways and wrong ways of doing things and easy ways and hard ways.

What are the problems? First, it could take days or even weeks to type in all of the many fifteen-place figures. More days or weeks might be required to check each table for possible typographical errors. Finally, such functions are usually limited to a narrow range of input arguments. For instance, a look-up table for the logarithms between 0 and 1 in increments of three decimal places (.001, .002, .003, and so on) would require 1001 different table elements, and such a table would not address values like .0015, which would require increments of .0001. If such a table were written into a function, more than 10,000 elements would be required for steps of .0001.

All of these problems must be dealt with. Some are inescapable, but others are not. First, functions that use look-up tables are necessarily limited in terms of range and increment of input arguments. However, this may not be a severe problem, assuming that such a function is to be used for a highly specialized and restricted purpose. It can be tailored to best address the specific needs of the programmer. Certainly, such a function would offer the most rapid access times, and accuracy could be anything you desire, since the values themselves would be typed in.

Second, the vast amounts of programming time can be overcome with a few tricks. To illustrate this, leaf through the next several pages, which contain a single function that will return the sine values for all numbers from 0 to 1 in increments of .001. Believe it or not, *this entire function was written in exactly 56 seconds on an IBM PC*. The method for accomplishing this admittedly unbelievable task is described at the end of the function:

```
double fstsin(x)
double x;
{

    int y;

    static double z[] = {
        { 0.00000000000000 }, { 0.00099999983333 }, { 0.00199999866667 },
        { 0.00299999550000 }, { 0.00399998933334 }, { 0.00499997916669 },
        { 0.00599996400006 }, { 0.00699994283347 }, { 0.00799991466694 },
        { 0.00899987850049 }, { 0.00999983333417 }, { 0.01099977816801 },
        { 0.01199971200207 }, { 0.01299963383643 }, { 0.01399954267115 },
        { 0.01499943750633 }, { 0.01599931734207 }, { 0.01699918117850 },
        { 0.01799902801575 }. { 0.01899885685397 }, { 0.01999866669333 },
```

```
{ 0.02099845653403 }, { 0.02199822537628 }, { 0.02299797222030 },
{ 0.02399769606635 }, { 0.02499739591471 }, { 0.02599707076568 },
{ 0.02699671961957 }, { 0.02799634147675 }, { 0.02899593533759 },
{ 0.02999550020250 }, { 0.03099503507190 }, { 0.03199453894628 },
{ 0.03299401082612 }, { 0.03399344971195 }, { 0.03499285460434 },
{ 0.03599222450387 }, { 0.03699155841118 }, { 0.03799085532694 },
{ 0.03899011425184 }, { 0.03998933418663 }, { 0.04098851413210 },
{ 0.04198765308905 }, { 0.04298675005835 }, { 0.04398580404091 },
{ 0.04498481403766 }, { 0.04598377904961 }, { 0.04698269807777 },
{ 0.04798157012325 }, { 0.04898039418716 }, { 0.04997916927068 },
{ 0.05097789437503 }, { 0.05197656850150 }, { 0.05297519065140 },
{ 0.05397375982611 }, { 0.05497227502707 }, { 0.05597073525576 },
{ 0.05696913951371 }, { 0.05796748680254 }, { 0.05896577612388 },
{ 0.05996400647944 }, { 0.06096217687101 }, { 0.06196028630041 },
{ 0.06295833376952 }, { 0.06395631828031 }, { 0.06495423883478 },
{ 0.06595209443502 }, { 0.06694988408317 }, { 0.06794760678145 },
{ 0.06894526153212 }, { 0.06994284733753 }, { 0.07094036320011 },
{ 0.07193780812232 }, { 0.07293518110674 }, { 0.07393248115598 },
{ 0.07492970727274 }, { 0.07592685845981 }, { 0.07692393372002 },
{ 0.07792093205630 }, { 0.07891785247166 }, { 0.07991469396917 },
{ 0.08091145555200 }, { 0.08190813622337 }, { 0.08290473498662 },
{ 0.08390125084514 }, { 0.08489768280242 }, { 0.08589402986202 },
{ 0.08689029102759 }, { 0.08788646530289 }, { 0.08888255169172 },
{ 0.08987854919801 }, { 0.09087445682576 }, { 0.09187027357906 },
{ 0.09286599846209 }, { 0.09386163047914 }, { 0.09485716863456 },
{ 0.09585261193282 }, { 0.09684795937847 }, { 0.09784320997618 },
{ 0.09883836273068 }, { 0.09983341664683 }, { 0.10082837072957 },
{ 0.10182322398395 }, { 0.10281797541511 }, { 0.10381262402830 },
{ 0.10480716882888 }, { 0.10580160882230 }, { 0.10679594301412 },
{ 0.10779017041001 }, { 0.10878429001573 }, { 0.10977830083717 },
{ 0.11077220188033 }, { 0.11176599215129 }, { 0.11275967065626 },
{ 0.11375323640158 }, { 0.11474668839366 }, { 0.11574002563907 },
{ 0.11673324714447 }, { 0.11772635191662 }, { 0.11871933896244 },
{ 0.11971220728892 }, { 0.12070495590321 }, { 0.12169758381255 },
{ 0.12269009002432 }, { 0.12368247354600 }, { 0.12467473338523 },
{ 0.12566686854973 }, { 0.12665887804737 }, { 0.12765076088615 },

{ 0.12864251607417 }, { 0.12963414261969 }, { 0.13062563953108 },
{ 0.13161700581684 }, { 0.13260824045561 }, { 0.13359934254614 },
{ 0.13459031100735 }, { 0.13558114487825 }, { 0.13657184316802 },
{ 0.13756240488596 }, { 0.13855282904151 }, { 0.13954311464424 },
{ 0.14053326070386 }, { 0.14152326623024 }, { 0.14251313023336 },
{ 0.14350285172336 }, { 0.14449242971053 }, { 0.14548186320527 },
{ 0.14647115121817 }, { 0.14746029275992 }, { 0.14844928684140 },
{ 0.14943813247360 }, { 0.15042682866768 }, { 0.15141537443494 },
{ 0.15240376878685 }, { 0.15339201073499 }, { 0.15438009929114 },
{ 0.15536803346721 }, { 0.15635581227525 }, { 0.15734343472749 },
{ 0.15833089983631 }, { 0.15931820661425 }, { 0.16030535407399 },
{ 0.16129234122839 }, { 0.16227916709046 }, { 0.16326583607338 },
{ 0.16425233099048 }, { 0.16523866705527 }, { 0.16622483788140 },
{ 0.16721084248270 }, { 0.16819667987318 }, { 0.16918234906700 },
{ 0.17016784907847 }, { 0.17115317892212 }, { 0.17213833761260 },
{ 0.17312332416475 }, { 0.17410813759360 }, { 0.17509277691450 },
{ 0.17607724114228 }, { 0.17706152929301 }, { 0.17804564038223 },
{ 0.17902957342582 }, { 0.18001332743986 }, { 0.18099690144058 },
{ 0.18198029444442 }, { 0.18296350546797 }, { 0.18394653352804 },
{ 0.18492937764159 }, { 0.18591203682578 }, { 0.18689451009794 },
{ 0.18787679647561 }, { 0.18885889497650 }, { 0.18984080461851 },
{ 0.19082252441973 }, { 0.19180405339845 }, { 0.19278539057312 },
{ 0.19376653496242 }, { 0.19474748558520 }, { 0.19572824146052 },
{ 0.19670880160760 }, { 0.19768916504591 }, { 0.19866933079506 },
{ 0.19964929787490 }, { 0.20062906530546 }, { 0.20160863210697 },
{ 0.20258799729986 }, { 0.20356715990478 }, { 0.20454611894255 },
{ 0.20552487343422 }, { 0.20650342240103 }, { 0.20748176486444 },
{ 0.20845989984610 }, { 0.20943782636788 }, { 0.21041554345185 },
{ 0.21139305012029 }, { 0.21237034539570 }, { 0.21334742830078 },
{ 0.21432429785845 }, { 0.21530095309185 }, { 0.21627739302430 },
{ 0.21725361667939 }, { 0.21822962308087 }, { 0.21920541125275 },
{ 0.22018098021923 }, { 0.22115632900476 }, { 0.22213145663397 },
```

(continued)

```
{ 0.22310636213175 },  { 0.22408104452318 },  { 0.22505550283358 },
{ 0.22602973608850 },  { 0.22700374331371 },  { 0.22797752353519 },
{ 0.22895107577916 },  { 0.22992439907208 },  { 0.23089749244062 },
{ 0.23187035491169 },  { 0.23284298551242 },  { 0.23381538327018 },
{ 0.23478754721258 },  { 0.23575947636745 },  { 0.23673116976287 },
{ 0.23770262642713 },  { 0.23867384538879 },  { 0.23964482567663 },
{ 0.24061556631966 },  { 0.24158606634714 },  { 0.24255632478857 },
{ 0.24352634067370 },  { 0.24449611303251 },  { 0.24546564089523 },
{ 0.24643492329233 },  { 0.24740395925452 },  { 0.24837274781278 },
{ 0.24934128799831 },  { 0.25030957884257 },  { 0.25127761937727 },
{ 0.25224540863438 },  { 0.25321294564610 },  { 0.25418022944489 },
{ 0.25514725906347 },  { 0.25611403353482 },  { 0.25708055189216 },
{ 0.25804681316896 },  { 0.25901281639897 },  { 0.25997856061619 },
{ 0.26094404485487 },  { 0.26190926814952 },  { 0.26287422953493 },
{ 0.26383892804614 },  { 0.26480336271843 },  { 0.26576753258739 },
{ 0.26673143668883 },  { 0.26769507405886 },  { 0.26865844373384 },
{ 0.26962154475040 },  { 0.27058437614543 },  { 0.27154693695611 },
{ 0.27250922621988 },  { 0.27347124297444 },  { 0.27443298625779 },
{ 0.27539445510817 },  { 0.27635564856411 },  { 0.27731656566444 },
{ 0.27827720544822 },  { 0.27923756695481 },  { 0.28019764922387 },
{ 0.28115745129529 },  { 0.28211697220929 },  { 0.28307621100635 },
{ 0.28403516672721 },  { 0.28499383841293 },  { 0.28595222510484 },
{ 0.28691032584454 },  { 0.28786813967394 },  { 0.28882566563523 },
{ 0.28978290277088 },  { 0.29073985012364 },  { 0.29169650673658 },

{ 0.29265287165304 },  { 0.29360894391665 },  { 0.29456472257135 },
{ 0.29552020666134 },  { 0.29647539523115 },  { 0.29743028732559 },
{ 0.29838488198977 },  { 0.29933917826909 },  { 0.30029317520926 },
{ 0.30124687185628 },  { 0.30220026725645 },  { 0.30315336045638 },
{ 0.30410615050297 },  { 0.30505863644344 },  { 0.30601081732530 },
{ 0.30696269219637 },  { 0.30791426010477 },  { 0.30886552009893 },
{ 0.30981647122760 },  { 0.31076711253983 },  { 0.31171744308497 },
{ 0.31266746191269 },  { 0.31361716807297 },  { 0.31456656061612 },
{ 0.31551563859273 },  { 0.31646440105372 },  { 0.31741284705035 },
{ 0.31836097563415 },  { 0.31930878585700 },  { 0.32025627677109 },
{ 0.32120344742894 },  { 0.32215029688336 },  { 0.32309682418751 },
{ 0.32404302839487 },  { 0.32498890855922 },  { 0.32593446373470 },
{ 0.32687969297573 },  { 0.32782459533710 },  { 0.32876916987390 },
{ 0.32971341564156 },  { 0.33065733169583 },  { 0.33160091709280 },
{ 0.33254417088888 },  { 0.33348709214081 },  { 0.33442967990569 },
{ 0.33537193324090 },  { 0.33631385120422 },  { 0.33725543285371 },
{ 0.33819667724779 },  { 0.33913758344523 },  { 0.34007815050511 },
{ 0.34101837748687 },  { 0.34195826345028 },  { 0.34289780745545 },
{ 0.34383700856285 },  { 0.34477586583326 },  { 0.34571437832784 },
{ 0.34665254510807 },  { 0.34759036523578 },  { 0.34852783777316 },
{ 0.34946496178273 },  { 0.35040173632736 },  { 0.35133816047029 },
{ 0.35227423327509 },  { 0.35320995380568 },  { 0.35414532112635 },
{ 0.35508033430173 },  { 0.35601499239680 },  { 0.35694929447691 },
{ 0.35788323960700 },  { 0.35881682685539 },  { 0.35975005528623 },
{ 0.36068292396704 },  { 0.36161543196496 },  { 0.36254757834748 },
{ 0.36347936218245 },  { 0.36441078253809 },  { 0.36534183848297 },
{ 0.36627252908605 },  { 0.36720285341663 },  { 0.36813281054438 },
{ 0.36906239953936 },  { 0.36999161947196 },  { 0.37092046941298 },
{ 0.37184894843356 },  { 0.37277705560522 },  { 0.37370478999986 },
{ 0.37463215068974 },  { 0.37555913674750 },  { 0.37648574724616 },
{ 0.37741198125059 },  { 0.37833783786008 },  { 0.37926331612326 },
{ 0.38018841512316 },  { 0.38111313393468 },  { 0.38203747163309 },
{ 0.38296142729406 },  { 0.38388499999364 },  { 0.38480818880825 },
{ 0.38573099281470 },  { 0.38665341109019 },  { 0.38757544271230 },
{ 0.38849708675900 },  { 0.38941834230865 },  { 0.39033920843999 },
{ 0.39125968423215 },  { 0.39217976876466 },  { 0.39309946111744 },
{ 0.39401876037078 },  { 0.39493766560540 },  { 0.39585617590238 },
{ 0.39677429034323 },  { 0.39769200800981 },  { 0.39860932798442 },
{ 0.39952624934974 },  { 0.40044277118884 },  { 0.40135889258520 },
{ 0.40227461262270 },  { 0.40318993038563 },  { 0.40410484495865 },
{ 0.40501935542687 },  { 0.40593346087576 },  { 0.40684716039123 },
{ 0.40776045305957 },  { 0.40867333796749 },  { 0.40958581420211 },
{ 0.41049788085095 },  { 0.41140953700194 },  { 0.41232078174342 },
```

```
( 0.41323161416417 ), ( 0.41414203335333 ), ( 0.41505203840049 ),
( 0.41596162839565 ), ( 0.41687080242921 ), ( 0.41777955959201 ),
( 0.41868789897528 ), ( 0.41959581967069 ), ( 0.42050332077031 ),
( 0.42141040136665 ), ( 0.42231706055262 ), ( 0.42322329742157 ),
( 0.42412911106725 ), ( 0.42503450058386 ), ( 0.42593946506600 ),
( 0.42684400360871 ), ( 0.42774811530746 ), ( 0.42865179925812 ),
( 0.42955505455703 ), ( 0.43045788030091 ), ( 0.43136027558695 ),
( 0.43226223951275 ), ( 0.43316377117634 ), ( 0.43406486967620 ),
( 0.43496553411123 ), ( 0.43586576358076 ), ( 0.43676555718456 ),
( 0.43766491402284 ), ( 0.43856383319625 ), ( 0.43946231380585 ),
( 0.44036035495318 ), ( 0.44125795574019 ), ( 0.44215511526929 ),
( 0.44305183264330 ), ( 0.44394810696552 ), ( 0.44484393733967 ),
( 0.44573932286992 ), ( 0.44663426266088 ), ( 0.44752875581762 ),

( 0.44842280144563 ), ( 0.44931639865089 ), ( 0.45020954653978 ),
( 0.45110224421917 ), ( 0.45199449079634 ), ( 0.45288628537907 ),
( 0.45377762707555 ), ( 0.45466851499443 ), ( 0.45555894824484 ),
( 0.45644892593634 ), ( 0.45733844717896 ), ( 0.45822751108316 ),
( 0.45911611675989 ), ( 0.46000426332054 ), ( 0.46089194987697 ),
( 0.46177917554148 ), ( 0.46266593942686 ), ( 0.46355224064634 ),
( 0.46443807831361 ), ( 0.46532345154285 ), ( 0.46620835944867 ),
( 0.46709280114618 ), ( 0.46797677575092 ), ( 0.46886028237892 ),
( 0.46974332014668 ), ( 0.47062588817116 ), ( 0.47150798556979 ),
( 0.47238961146047 ), ( 0.47327076496158 ), ( 0.47415144519197 ),
( 0.47503165127095 ), ( 0.47591138231832 ), ( 0.47679063745435 ),
( 0.47766941579977 ), ( 0.47854771647583 ), ( 0.47942553860420 ),
( 0.48030288130708 ), ( 0.48117974370712 ), ( 0.48205612492745 ),
( 0.48293202409170 ), ( 0.48380744032396 ), ( 0.48468237274882 ),
( 0.48555682047136 ), ( 0.48643079254842 ), ( 0.48730425843212 ),
( 0.48817724688291 ), ( 0.48904974715649 ), ( 0.48992175838037 ),
( 0.49079327968253 ), ( 0.49166431019146 ), ( 0.49253484903611 ),
( 0.49340489534595 ), ( 0.49427444825095 ), ( 0.49514350688153 ),
( 0.49601207036865 ), ( 0.49688013784374 ), ( 0.49774770843873 ),
( 0.49861478128606 ), ( 0.49948135551864 ), ( 0.50034743026991 ),
( 0.50121300467380 ), ( 0.50207807786472 ), ( 0.50294264897760 ),
( 0.50380671714788 ), ( 0.50467028151148 ), ( 0.50553334120485 ),
( 0.50639589536491 ), ( 0.50725794312912 ), ( 0.50811948363543 ),
( 0.50898051602230 ), ( 0.50984103942870 ), ( 0.51070105299409 ),
( 0.51156055585848 ), ( 0.51241954716236 ), ( 0.51327802604603 ),
( 0.51413599165311 ), ( 0.51499344312355 ), ( 0.51585037960059 ),
( 0.51670680022729 ), ( 0.51756270414723 ), ( 0.51841809050452 ),
( 0.51927295844375 ), ( 0.52012730711007 ), ( 0.52098113564913 ),
( 0.52183444320709 ), ( 0.52268722893066 ), ( 0.52353949196704 ),
( 0.52439123146397 ), ( 0.52524244656971 ), ( 0.52609313643305 ),
( 0.52694330020330 ), ( 0.52779293703029 ), ( 0.52864204606439 ),
( 0.52949062645649 ), ( 0.53033867335800 ), ( 0.53118619792088 ),
( 0.53203318729761 ), ( 0.53287964464120 ), ( 0.53372556910518 ),
( 0.53457095984364 ), ( 0.53541581601118 ), ( 0.53626013676296 ),
( 0.53710392125464 ), ( 0.53794716864244 ), ( 0.53878987808312 ),
( 0.53963204873397 ), ( 0.54047367975281 ), ( 0.54131477029802 ),
( 0.54215531952851 ), ( 0.54299532660371 ), ( 0.54383479068364 ),
( 0.54467371092883 ), ( 0.54551208650034 ), ( 0.54634991655982 ),
( 0.54718720026942 ), ( 0.54802393679187 ), ( 0.54886012529043 ),
( 0.54969576492891 ), ( 0.55053085487167 ), ( 0.55136539428362 ),
( 0.55219938233023 ), ( 0.55303281817749 ), ( 0.55386570099199 ),
( 0.55469802994083 ), ( 0.55552980419169 ), ( 0.55636102291278 ),
( 0.55719168527291 ), ( 0.55802179044139 ), ( 0.55885133758813 ),
( 0.55968032588358 ), ( 0.56050875449874 ), ( 0.56133662260521 ),
( 0.56216392937509 ), ( 0.56299067398109 ), ( 0.56381685559647 ),
( 0.56464247339504 ), ( 0.56546752655118 ), ( 0.56629201423984 ),
( 0.56711593563653 ), ( 0.56793928991734 ), ( 0.56876207625890 ),
( 0.56958429383843 ), ( 0.57040594183372 ), ( 0.57122701942312 ),
( 0.57204752578554 ), ( 0.57286746010048 ), ( 0.57368682154801 ),
( 0.57450560930877 ), ( 0.57532382256397 ), ( 0.57614146049539 ),
( 0.57695852228540 ), ( 0.57777500711693 ), ( 0.57859091417351 ),
( 0.57940624263922 ), ( 0.58022099169873 ), ( 0.58103516053731 ),
( 0.58184874834077 ), ( 0.58266175429553 ), ( 0.58347417758858 ),
( 0.58428601740751 ), ( 0.58509727294046 ), ( 0.58590794337619 ),
```

(continued)

```
( 0.58671802790403 ),   ( 0.58752752571389 ),   ( 0.58833643599627 ),
( 0.58914475794227 ),   ( 0.58995249074356 ),   ( 0.59075963359240 ),
( 0.59156618568166 ),   ( 0.59237214620479 ),   ( 0.59317751435581 ),
( 0.59398228932938 ),   ( 0.59478647032070 ),   ( 0.59559005652560 ),
( 0.59639304714049 ),   ( 0.59719544136239 ),   ( 0.59799723838890 ),
( 0.59879843741822 ),   ( 0.59959903764915 ),   ( 0.60039903828109 ),
( 0.60119843851404 ),   ( 0.60199723754861 ),   ( 0.60279543458598 ),
( 0.60359302882798 ),   ( 0.60439001947699 ),   ( 0.60518640573604 ),
( 0.60598218680873 ),   ( 0.60677736189928 ),   ( 0.60757193021253 ),
( 0.60836589095389 ),   ( 0.60915924332941 ),   ( 0.60995198654575 ),
( 0.61074411981014 ),   ( 0.61153564233047 ),   ( 0.61232655331520 ),
( 0.61311685197343 ),   ( 0.61390653751487 ),   ( 0.61469560914981 ),
( 0.61548406608920 ),   ( 0.61627190754457 ),   ( 0.61705913272809 ),
( 0.61784574085252 ),   ( 0.61863173113127 ),   ( 0.61941710277833 ),
( 0.62020185500835 ),   ( 0.62098598703656 ),   ( 0.62176949807884 ),
( 0.62255238735167 ),   ( 0.62333465407216 ),   ( 0.62411629745805 ),
( 0.62489731672770 ),   ( 0.62567771110008 ),   ( 0.62645747979481 ),
( 0.62723662203210 ),   ( 0.62801513703283 ),   ( 0.62879302401847 ),
( 0.62957028221114 ),   ( 0.63034691083358 ),   ( 0.63112290910916 ),
( 0.63189827626189 ),   ( 0.63267301151639 ),   ( 0.63344711409793 ),
( 0.63422058323241 ),   ( 0.63499341814636 ),   ( 0.63576561806695 ),
( 0.63653718222197 ),   ( 0.63730810983986 ),   ( 0.63807840014969 ),
( 0.63884805238118 ),   ( 0.63961706576467 ),   ( 0.64038543953115 ),
( 0.64115317291224 ),   ( 0.64192026514021 ),   ( 0.64268671544797 ),
( 0.64345252306906 ),   ( 0.64421768723769 ),   ( 0.64498220718869 ),
( 0.64574608215753 ),   ( 0.64650931138034 ),   ( 0.64727189409389 ),
( 0.64803382953561 ),   ( 0.64879511694355 ),   ( 0.64955575555642 ),
( 0.65031574461360 ),   ( 0.65107508335508 ),   ( 0.65183377102154 ),
( 0.65259180685428 ),   ( 0.65334919009526 ),   ( 0.65410591998711 ),
( 0.65486199577310 ),   ( 0.65561741669714 ),   ( 0.65637218200382 ),
( 0.65712629093838 ),   ( 0.65787974749690 ),   ( 0.65863253667533 ),
( 0.65938467197147 ),   ( 0.66013614788300 ),   ( 0.66088696365844 ),
( 0.66163711854697 ),   ( 0.66238661179844 ),   ( 0.66313544266335 ),
( 0.66388361039287 ),   ( 0.66463111423884 ),   ( 0.66537795345375 ),
( 0.66612412729076 ),   ( 0.66686963500370 ),   ( 0.66761447584706 ),
( 0.66835864907600 ),   ( 0.66910215394634 ),   ( 0.66984498971459 ),
( 0.67058715563709 ),   ( 0.67132865097412 ),   ( 0.67206947498174 ),
( 0.67280962691994 ),   ( 0.67354910604857 ),   ( 0.67428791162815 ),
( 0.67502604291987 ),   ( 0.67576349918561 ),   ( 0.67650027968790 ),
( 0.67723638368997 ),   ( 0.67797181045572 ),   ( 0.67870655924970 ),
( 0.67944062933719 ),   ( 0.68017401998411 ),   ( 0.68090673045706 ),
( 0.68163876002333 ),   ( 0.68237010795091 ),   ( 0.68310077350843 ),
( 0.68383075596524 ),   ( 0.68456005459134 ),   ( 0.68528866865746 ),
( 0.68601659743495 ),   ( 0.68674384019591 ),   ( 0.68747039621309 ),
( 0.68819626475992 ),   ( 0.68892144511055 ),   ( 0.68964593653979 ),
( 0.69036973832315 ),   ( 0.69109284973684 ),   ( 0.69181527005772 ),
( 0.69253699856340 ),   ( 0.69325803453214 ),   ( 0.69397837724290 ),
( 0.69469802597534 ),   ( 0.69541698000981 ),   ( 0.69613523862736 ),
( 0.69685280110973 ),   ( 0.69756966673935 ),   ( 0.69828583479937 ),
( 0.69900130457361 ),   ( 0.69971607534660 ),   ( 0.70043014640358 ),
( 0.70114351703047 ),   ( 0.70185618651390 ),   ( 0.70256815414120 ),
( 0.70327941920041 ),   ( 0.70398998098026 ),   ( 0.70469983877018 ),
( 0.70540899186033 ),   ( 0.70611743954154 ),   ( 0.70682518110537 ),
( 0.70753221584407 ),   ( 0.70823854305063 ),   ( 0.70894416201069 ),
( 0.70964907204266 ),   ( 0.71035327241761 ),   ( 0.71105676243935 ),
( 0.71175954140438 ),   ( 0.71246160860993 ),   ( 0.71316296335394 ),
( 0.71386360493504 ),   ( 0.71456353265259 ),   ( 0.71526274580667 ),
( 0.71596124369807 ),   ( 0.71665902562828 ),   ( 0.71735609089952 ),
( 0.71805243881474 ),   ( 0.71874806867757 ),   ( 0.71944297979240 ),
( 0.72013717146430 ),   ( 0.72083064299910 ),   ( 0.72152339370331 ),
( 0.72221542288419 ),   ( 0.72290672984970 ),   ( 0.72359731390855 ),
( 0.72428717437014 ),   ( 0.72497631054462 ),   ( 0.72566472174285 ),
( 0.72635240727642 ),   ( 0.72703936645764 ),   ( 0.72772559859955 ),
( 0.72841110301593 ),   ( 0.72909587902126 ),   ( 0.72977992593078 ),
( 0.73046324306043 ),   ( 0.73114582972690 ),   ( 0.73182768524760 ),
( 0.73250880894067 ),   ( 0.73318920012500 ),   ( 0.73386885812019 ),
( 0.73454778224658 ),   ( 0.73522597182525 ),   ( 0.73590342617801 ),
( 0.73658014462740 ),   ( 0.73725612649672 ),   ( 0.73793137110996 ),
```

```
        { 0.73860587779190 },  { 0.73927964586802 },  { 0.73995267466456 },
        { 0.74062496350848 },  { 0.74129651172750 },  { 0.74196731865007 },
        { 0.74263738360539 },  { 0.74330670592338 },  { 0.74397528493473 },
        { 0.74464311997086 },  { 0.74531021036393 },  { 0.74597655544685 },
        { 0.74664215455328 },  { 0.74730700701761 },  { 0.74797111217500 },
        { 0.74863446936134 },  { 0.74929707791327 },  { 0.74995893716819 },
        { 0.75062004646423 },  { 0.75128040514029 },  { 0.75194001253601 },
        { 0.75259886799178 },  { 0.75325697084874 },  { 0.75391432044879 },
        { 0.75457091613459 },  { 0.75522675724953 },  { 0.75588184313778 },
        { 0.75653617314425 },  { 0.75718974661460 },  { 0.75784256289528 },
        { 0.75849462133345 },  { 0.75914592127707 },  { 0.75979646207483 },
        { 0.76044624307619 },  { 0.76109526363137 },  { 0.76174352309135 },
        { 0.76239102080787 },  { 0.76303775613343 },  { 0.76368372842130 },
        { 0.76432893702551 },  { 0.76497338130084 },  { 0.76561706060285 },
        { 0.76625997428787 },  { 0.76690212171298 },  { 0.76754350223603 },
        { 0.76818411521564 },  { 0.76882396001120 },  { 0.76946303598286 },
        { 0.77010134249156 },  { 0.77073887889897 },  { 0.77137564456757 },
        { 0.77201163886059 },  { 0.77264686114203 },  { 0.77328131077648 },
        { 0.77391498713008 },  { 0.77454788956856 },  { 0.77518001745921 },
        { 0.77581137016992 },  { 0.77644194706931 },  { 0.77707174752682 },
        { 0.77770077091265 },  { 0.77832901659778 },  { 0.77895648395395 },
        { 0.77958317235370 },  { 0.78020908117035 },  { 0.78083420977798 },
        { 0.78145855755147 },  { 0.78208212388646 },  { 0.78270490809939 },
        { 0.78332690962748 },  { 0.78394812782873 },  { 0.78456856208191 },
        { 0.78518821176660 },  { 0.78580707626314 },  { 0.78642515495267 },
        { 0.78704244721712 },  { 0.78765895243917 },  { 0.78827467000235 },
        { 0.78888959929092 },  { 0.78950373968995 },  { 0.79011709058531 },
        { 0.79072965136365 },  { 0.79134142141240 },  { 0.79195240011979 },
        { 0.79256258687485 },  { 0.79317198106740 },  { 0.79378058208802 },
        { 0.79438838932813 },  { 0.79499540217992 },  { 0.79560162003637 },
        { 0.79620704229126 },  { 0.79681166833918 },  { 0.79741549757550 },
        { 0.79801852939639 },  { 0.79862076319881 },  { 0.79922219838054 },
        { 0.79982283434014 },  { 0.80042267047697 },  { 0.80102170619119 },
        { 0.80161994088378 },  { 0.80221737395649 },  { 0.80281400481189 },
        { 0.80340983285336 },  { 0.80400485748506 },  { 0.80459907811197 },
        { 0.80519249413987 },  { 0.80578510497534 },  { 0.80637691002577 },
        { 0.80696790869936 },  { 0.80755810040511 },  { 0.80814748455283 },
        { 0.80873606055313 },  { 0.80932382781744 },  { 0.80991078575798 },
        { 0.81049693378781 },  { 0.81108227132077 },  { 0.81166679777153 },
        { 0.81225051255556 },  { 0.81283341508914 },  { 0.81341550478937 },
        { 0.81399678107417 },  { 0.81457724336226 },  { 0.81515689107317 },
        { 0.81573572362725 },  { 0.81631374044568 },  { 0.81689094095044 },
        { 0.81746732456433 },  { 0.81804289071096 },  { 0.81861763881476 },
        { 0.81919156830100 },  { 0.81976467859573 },  { 0.82033696912586 },
        { 0.82090843931908 },  { 0.82147908860394 },  { 0.82204891640977 },
        { 0.82261792216676 },  { 0.82318610530589 },  { 0.82375346525899 },
        { 0.82432000145868 },  { 0.82488571333845 },  { 0.82545060033257 },
        { 0.82601466187616 },  { 0.82657789740516 },  { 0.82714030635633 },
        { 0.82770188816726 },  { 0.82826264227637 },  { 0.82882256812291 },
        { 0.82938166514695 },  { 0.82993993278939 },  { 0.83049737049197 },
        { 0.83105397769952 },  { 0.83160975384862 },  { 0.83216469839031 },
        { 0.83271881076736 },  { 0.83327209042568 },  { 0.83382453681197 },
        { 0.83437614937380 },  { 0.83492692755954 },  { 0.83547687081843 },
        { 0.83602597860052 },  { 0.83657425035670 },  { 0.83712168553870 },
        { 0.83766828359908 },  { 0.83821404399125 },  { 0.83875896616944 },
        { 0.83930304958874 },  { 0.83984629370506 },  { 0.84038869797516 },
        { 0.84093026185662 },  { 0.84147098480790 }
    };

    y = (x / 0.00100) - (0.00000 / 0.00100);

    return(z[y]);

}
```

Obviously, this is a very long function, but it is extremely simple, at least in terms of mathematics. The great majority of this function is devoted to specifying the 1001 sine values for the range of 0 to 1 in increments of 0.001. The function argument (x) is divided by the increment (0.00100) minus the starting value of the table (0.00000) divided again by the increment. If the table had started with the sine of 0.8, then a value of 0.801 would access the second array element. In other words, z[y] in the return statement would be equal to z[1], which is the second element, z[0] being the first.

As I stated just before listing the source code of this function, this entire function was written from start to finish in less than one minute! It was written entirely by calling another function, called mkfunc(), whose sole purpose is to write other functions.

Lest you think I have hit on some magical means of writing long, complex functions, I should note that every value found in the fstsin() table was generated by the sin() function discussed earlier. You will recall that this was a fast, accurate function in itself, requiring approximately 8 seconds for 1000 calls. The magic function, mkfunc(), simply called sin() 1001 times and caused the return to be printed to an ASCII file. So the magic is somewhat diluted by the fact that in order to generate a function using mkfunc(), you must also have another function that can return the values to be printed in that table.

There is still a bit of magic to it, however, because mkfunc() requires only five arguments: first, the name of the C file that is to be created; second, the name of the function to be called in order to return the table values—in this case, sin(); third and fourth, the starting and ending values that will be fed to the function named in the second argument; and finally, a step value, which names the steps that will be used to increment between the starting value and the ending value. Most important is the fact that mkfunc() writes the complete function in a form that is ready to be compiled. Once mkfunc() has been called, all you do is compile the file it generates. You don't have to write a single line of source code! The source code for mkfunc() is as follows:

```
#include <stdio.h>
mkfunc(n, f, start, end, step)
char *n;
double (*f)(), start, end, step;
{
        FILE *fp, *fopen();
        char funcname[12];
        double x;
        int i, ct;

        ct = i = 0;
        fp = fopen(n, "w");

        while (*n !='.')
                funcname[i++] = *n++;

        funcname[i] = '\0';
```

```
fprintf(fp, "double %s(x)\n", funcname);
fprintf(fp, "double x;\n{\n\n");
fprintf(fp, "    int y;\n\n");
fprintf(fp, "    static double z[] = {\n");
fprintf(fp, "          ");

for (x = start; x < end; x += step) {
     fprintf(fp, "{ %.14f }, ", (*f)(x));
     ++ct;
     if (ct == 3) {
          ct = 0;
          fprintf(fp, "\n               ");
     }

}

fprintf(fp, "{ %.14f }\n      };\n\n", (*f)(end));

fprintf(fp, "     y = (x / %.5f) - (%.5f / %.5f);\n\n", step,
start, step);
fprintf(fp, "     return(z[y]);\n\n}");

fclose(fp);
```

}

Here, variable n is a char * pointer that is the name of the file to which the
function is to be written. Variable f is another pointer that has the memory address
of the function that will be used to get values for the table. The meanings of the
remaining variables are obvious from their names.

The following program was used to call mkfunc(), which, in turn, generated
fstsin() with its long look-up table:

```
main()
{

     double sin();

     mkfunc("fstsin.c", sin, 0.0, 1.0, .001);

}
```

It can be seen that the name of the file that will contain the function to be
generated is "fstsin.c". It is very important to include the extension, because
mkfunc() uses the decimal point as a key. The function will automatically be named
double fstsin() or anything else that precedes the decimal point.

The function that will be used to get the table values is sin(). It is declared in
the calling program, and its name is the second argument to mkfunc(). Notice that
the following parentheses are not a part of this argument and that sin is treated as a

variable—that is, there are no quotation marks surrounding it. This is a must proto-
col when passing arguments to this function.

The remainder of the arguments are constants. The value 0.0 marks the starting value for the table. This means that the first sine value printed in the table will be
the sine of 0.0. The next constant argument is 1.0. This marks the last value whose
sine will appear in the table. The last argument names the steps the sine values will
take. Thus, the value .001 means that the sine of all values from 0 to 1 will be a part
of the table in increments of .001. So the first sine value is for 0, the second for
.001, the third for .002 and so on, up to a value of 1.0.

When these values are passed to mkfunc(), they are used to open a file, to set
up a pointer to a function (*f)() = = sin(), and to determine the starting, ending, and
step values of a for loop. Once the file has been opened, a while statement extracts
the function name from the file name. It does this by taking all characters up to the
decimal point.

From here on, a few program lines write C source code to the file, just as you
might type them in on the keyboard. A static double array is declared in source
code. Then, the for loop begins stepping through the range of values specified in the
function arguments. On each pass, the sine of the loop value is written to the file in a
format that is in accordance with correct C programming.

When the table is complete, the proper termination brace and semicolon is
added, and the formula for determining the value of int y is created by using the
value of variables start and step.

Variable y will determine which array element is accessed, based on some
future argument, still in the process of creation, that will be passed to this function.
The return statement line is written to the file next, followed by the function's
closing brace.

Now fclose is called to close the file that contains the function that was created
by another function. This entire process took less than a minute to create fstsin().
The beauty of it lies in the fact that mkfunc() can be used to create any table using
any function that accepts a single argument. I might just as well have used exp(),
cos(), arctan(), log(), or any of the other functions discussed earlier.

For instance, the following C program calls mkfunc() to create a table of exponents using exp(). The table will list the exponents over a range of 0.700 to 0.900 in
increments of .001:

```
main()
{

    double exp();

    mkfunc("fstexp.c", exp, 0.7, 0.9, 0.001);

}
```

This is an extremely simple calling procedure. First, exp() is declared a double. Second, mkfunc() is called with the arguments that name the disk file (and function name), the function used to compile the table (exp), and the start, end, and step values. The function created by this call is fstexp():

```
double fstexp(x)
double x;
{

    int y;

    static double z[] = {
        { 2.01375270747047 },  { 2.01576746739001 },  { 2.01778424307718 },
        { 2.01980303654876 },  { 2.02182384982354 },  { 2.02384668492235 },
        { 2.02587154386800 },  { 2.02789842868537 },  { 2.02992734140134 },
        { 2.03195828404482 },  { 2.03399125864675 },  { 2.03602626724011 },
        { 2.03806331185990 },  { 2.04010239454318 },  { 2.04214351732902 },
        { 2.04418668225856 },  { 2.04623189137494 },  { 2.04827914672338 },
        { 2.05032845035114 },  { 2.05237980430753 },  { 2.05443321064389 },
        { 2.05648867141363 },  { 2.05854618867221 },  { 2.06060576447715 },
        { 2.06266740088803 },  { 2.06473109996649 },  { 2.06679686377621 },
        { 2.06886469438297 },  { 2.07093459385460 },  { 2.07300656426099 },
        { 2.07508060767412 },  { 2.07715672616803 },  { 2.07923492181884 },
        { 2.08131519670475 },  { 2.08339755290602 },  { 2.08548199250503 },
        { 2.08756851758620 },  { 2.08965713023606 },  { 2.09174783254322 },
        { 2.09384062659839 },  { 2.09593551449436 },  { 2.09803249832603 },
        { 2.10013158019036 },  { 2.10223276218645 },  { 2.10433604641548 },
        { 2.10644143498073 },  { 2.10854892998759 },  { 2.11065853354355 },
        { 2.11277024775823 },  { 2.11488407474332 },  { 2.11700001661267 },
        { 2.11911807548222 },  { 2.12123825347001 },  { 2.12336055269624 },
        { 2.12548497528319 },  { 2.12761152335530 },  { 2.12974019903911 },
        { 2.13187100446329 },  { 2.13400394175866 },  { 2.13613901305814 },
        { 2.13827622049682 },  { 2.14041556621189 },  { 2.14255705234272 },
        { 2.14470068103077 },  { 2.14684645441968 },  { 2.14899437465522 },
        { 2.15114444388532 },  { 2.15329666426004 },  { 2.15545103793161 },
        { 2.15760756705439 },  { 2.15976625378492 },  { 2.16192710028188 },
        { 2.16409010870612 },  { 2.16625528122066 },  { 2.16842261999065 },
        { 2.17059212718344 },  { 2.17276380496855 },  { 2.17493765551764 },
        { 2.17711368100456 },  { 2.17929188360535 },  { 2.18147226549820 },
        { 2.18365482886350 },  { 2.18583957588381 },  { 2.18802650874388 },
        { 2.19021562963064 },  { 2.19240694073322 },  { 2.19460044424291 },
        { 2.19679614235324 },  { 2.19899403725989 },  { 2.20119413116075 },
```

(continued)

```
( 2.20339642625594 ),  ( 2.20560092474773 ),  ( 2.20780762884063 ),
( 2.21001654074135 ),  ( 2.21222766265879 ),  ( 2.21444099680408 ),
( 2.21665654539054 ),  ( 2.21887431063374 ),  ( 2.22109429475144 ),
( 2.22331649996361 ),  ( 2.22554092849247 ),  ( 2.22776758256244 ),
( 2.22999646440018 ),  ( 2.23222757623458 ),  ( 2.23446092029673 ),
( 2.23669649881999 ),  ( 2.23893431403993 ),  ( 2.24117436819438 ),
( 2.24341666352338 ),  ( 2.24566120226923 ),  ( 2.24790798667647 ),
( 2.25015701899189 ),  ( 2.25240830146451 ),  ( 2.25466183634562 ),
( 2.25691762588875 ),  ( 2.25917567234970 ),  ( 2.26143597798651 ),
( 2.26369854505949 ),  ( 2.26596337583120 ),  ( 2.26823047256647 ),
( 2.27049983753241 ),  ( 2.27277147299837 ),  ( 2.27504538123599 ),
( 2.27732156451919 ),  ( 2.27960002512414 ),  ( 2.28188076532930 ),
( 2.28416378741542 ),  ( 2.28644909366552 ),  ( 2.28873668636490 ),
( 2.29102656780116 ),  ( 2.29331874026418 ),  ( 2.29561320604613 ),
( 2.29790996744148 ),  ( 2.30020902674699 ),  ( 2.30251038626171 ),
( 2.30481404828701 ),  ( 2.30712001512656 ),  ( 2.30942828908631 ),
( 2.31173887247454 ),  ( 2.31405176760183 ),  ( 2.31636697678109 ),
( 2.31868450232752 ),  ( 2.32100434655864 ),  ( 2.32332651179430 ),
( 2.32565100035667 ),  ( 2.32797781457024 ),  ( 2.33030695676181 ),
( 2.33263842926053 ),  ( 2.33497223439787 ),  ( 2.33730837450765 ),
( 2.33964685192599 ),  ( 2.34198766899138 ),  ( 2.34433082804464 ),
( 2.34667633142891 ),  ( 2.34902418148972 ),  ( 2.35137438057490 ),
( 2.35372693103466 ),  ( 2.35608183522155 ),  ( 2.35843909549047 ),
( 2.36079871419868 ),  ( 2.36316069370580 ),  ( 2.36552503637381 ),
( 2.36789174456705 ),  ( 2.37026082065224 ),  ( 2.37263226699844 ),
( 2.37500608597711 ),  ( 2.37738227996207 ),  ( 2.37976085132950 ),
( 2.38214180245798 ),  ( 2.38452513572846 ),  ( 2.38691085352428 ),
( 2.38929895823115 ),  ( 2.39168945223717 ),  ( 2.39408233793285 ),
( 2.39647761771107 ),  ( 2.39887529396710 ),  ( 2.40127536909862 ),
```

This function appears exactly as it was written by mkfunc(). This is the actual source code from the file this function created.

Notice that the assignment to variable y prior to the return statement takes the starting value for which the table was set up and the increment value to determine which table item will be accessed by a particular argument.

Some readers may wonder about the usefulness of a function that creates new functions, especially since it is mandatory to already have a function that can return the various values needed for the table. The whole concept behind mkfunc() is to develop look-up table functions that have greatly increased access speed compared to other functions that arrive at the same values through mathematic formulas. A function that can create complete look-up table functions that are ready to be compiled serves several purposes. First, it creates superfast, highly specialized improvements based on the return values of those slower functions. Second, it can quickly formulate look-up tables that are accurate to the precision provided by the existing function used to return those table values. These tables can then be quickly upgraded to better precision using a printed look-up table and a line editor to make additions or changes to the values already contained in the created function. As an example, assume that the log() function is used with mkfunc() to create a look-up table function that is accurate to ten decimal places, this being the accuracy of log(). Assume, also, that you need a table that is accurate to fifteen decimal places. Now, using a published look-up table that is accurate to fifteen decimal places, you simply edit the created function and add the five numbers to each table item from the published chart. This can still be quite time-consuming, but it is many times faster than typing in the complete values from scratch.

Look-up table functions are quite limited in the range of values they can accept as their arguments. An argument value must coincide with one of the values used in making the table originally. However, such functions are designed for specialized purposes. Many programs access math functions with a limited range of arguments. If they can be accurately determined and a reasonable range can be arrived at, a look-up table should always be the choice, assuming that execution speed and accuracy are of equal importance.

Functions in previous sections have used conversions to pull arguments into ranges acceptable to their various approximation routines. This can also apply to look-up table functions, although you must make certain that any conversions meet the range and step requirements. For instance, if a particular table is constructed in input steps of .001, a value of 1.0015 will fall between steps, and a wrong value will be returned. Sometimes, it's better to create look-up tables in much smaller steps—say, .0001—but this limits the range of values that can be practically contained in such a table. I have constructed table functions containing more than 10,000 items, but these are quite cumbersome, and some compilers may not be able to handle a function of this magnitude. Most practical table functions contain fewer than 2000 items.

Considering most programming demands from a realistic viewpoint, the precision and speed available from functions that use look-up tables are not often required. With the exception of some graphics applications, most programs written in C on microcomputers will be quite satisfactory using the function sets described previously. They are far more versatile than the ones discussed here, as they are not as limited in argument range. Most of the previous functions are quite fast and accurate and should serve the microcomputer programmer well in most applications. However, there may come a time when greater speed and precision are required. The knowledge gained from this section should aid you in writing the specialized functions needed to meet this demand.

SUMMARY

You may be satisfied with the math functions your present C programming environment already offers, and you may never have to resort to the functions presented in this chapter. However, there is a very good chance that as you continue to advance in C programming, there will come a time when faster or more accurate math functions are required.

On the other hand, if you have been stuck with a compiler that offers none of the complex math functions, the functions presented in this chapter can be copied right out of the book and put to work for you right away. It's not even necessary that you understand *how* they work—only that they do. They should be compatible with almost every full-range C compiler.

CHAPTER FIVE

Pointers and Memory Access

POINTER OPERATIONS

Pointer operations in C language are an area that generally tends to give the beginning programmer the most difficulty. Although pointers are used in BASIC, their implementation is hidden from the programmer. However, C language allows pointers to be specifically programmed and used to great advantage. Pointer operations in C are responsible for much of the versatility associated with this programming language.

Simply put, a pointer is a special type of variable that points to a specific place in memory. Typically, a pointer points to a part of memory where a value is stored or where one is to be stored. Remember, a pointer is not directly equal to any user-defined value; rather, it is the place in memory where such a value is stored.

In C, *character* pointers are used quite often. Such pointers are very similar in use to char arrays, which were discussed earlier. As a matter of fact, char pointers and char arrays may be treated as one and the same in many C operations.

The following program example shows how a character pointer is declared and used within a simple C program:

```
main()
{

    char *a;

    a = "hello";

    printf("%s\n", a);

}
```

First, variable a is declared a char pointer. This is done by using the unary operator, which is represented by an asterisk (*). The unary operator specifies a pointer, as opposed to a standard char variable. This special variable is now available to point to a specific place in memory, which will contain a *string* of values that represent printable characters (ASCII 0–255). The end of the string is signified by a null character (\0) just as it is when setting up a char array.

When a character pointer is declared, it points to a random location in memory. To make proper use of a pointer, it is necessary to give it something tangible to point to. In this case, the word "hello" is provided. This is done just as it would be done in BASIC, through the use of the assignment operator (=) and the string constant enclosed in double quotes.

Do not be misled into thinking that the pointer is somehow equal to the word "hello". It is *not*! Rather, a points to the location where the computer has stored the constant "hello". It should be remembered that a pointer must point to something that is already in existence. It differs from a standard variable in that it can hold nothing. It only points to something that is already stored in memory or to a memory location that has been set aside for future storage. Standard variables, when declared, have storage space set aside for them. For instance, an int variable automatically has 16 bits of storage set aside in memory when such a variable is declared, assuming the use of a standard MS-DOS microcomputer. However, no *storage* space is set aside for a pointer.

The constant "hello" is actually written into the program, and when this program is run, the computer must allocate a place in memory to store this constant. It is not important to know where the constant is stored, so long as we know that a points to that location. Notice that when the printf function is used, the pointer is treated just as though it were a char array variable. The pointer points to the memory location that contains the first character in the string "hello". All following memory locations are read sequentially until the null character is detected. This marks the end of the string, and printf is exited.

Let's examine pointers in more detail, using the foregoing program as an example. Assume that the constant "hello" is stored in RAM memory at location 15,000. This means that the letter h resides at 15,000 and the letters e, l, l, and o are found at 15,001, 15,002, 15,003, and 15,004, respectively. There is also one additional character, which is stored at 15,005. This is the null character (\0), which signifies the end of the character string in memory. Pointer a points to location 15,000, the start of the character string. When used to represent a string value (as opposed to each character that makes up the string), all memory locations from and including 15,000 are read until the null character is reached.

One can quickly see the relationship between character pointers and character arrays. This relationship is actual rather than symbolic, which is why character pointers and character arrays may be treated as one and the same in many C operations, especially those that involve functions that accept character strings as arguments.

However, character pointers and character arrays must also be thought of as completely different, in that one is a pointer with no storage space set aside and the other is a variable with a programmed amount of space set aside for storage. The following program does the same as the previous one; however, a char array is used instead of a pointer:

```
main()
{

    char a[10];

    strcpy(a, "hello");

    printf("%s\n", a);

}
```

Here, the strcpy function is used to copy "hello" into the storage location set aside specifically for the char array. From this point on, the access by printf is the same as before. We cannot make a direct assignment with a char array (through use of the assignment operator), as we did with the pointer. In this example, the constant "hello" is contained at one memory location and the storage space set aside for the char array is at another. In other words, the constant is copied into the storage area represented by the array. Using a pointer, no copying of storage area takes place. The pointer simply directs attention to the constant at its original place in memory.

The following is an example of improper use of a pointer:

```
main()
{

    char *a;                              WRONG

    strcpy(a, "hello");

    printf("%s\n", a);

}
```

This program mistakenly uses a pointer as though it were a char array. The strcpy function copies data from one memory location to another. This assumes that the target location is large enough in sequential memory spaces to hold whatever is obtained from the source. This works fine for char arrays, but remember that pointers do not have space automatically set aside. When first declared, they point to a random location in memory. A better way of thinking of this is to say that unassigned pointers can point to any place in memory, including certain areas that are already in use. An improper use of pointers, as the foregoing program demonstrates, could result in valuable memory locations being overwritten. This can cause the entire program to "crash." At worst, it can write over the portion of memory that designates disk files and cause them to be lost. Frequently, the program will run just fine. In such instances, the programmer has gotten off lucky, because the pointer was randomly directed to a safe area of memory.

Here is another program that shows improper use of a pointer:

```
main()
{

    char *a;

    gets(a);

    printf("%s\n", a);

}
```

In this example, the gets function is used to read the keyboard input. The intention here is to *assign* the pointer the value of the keyboard string. Again, you may get away with this if the declared pointer happens to access an unused portion of memory, but this is bad and potentially disastrous programming. Some compilers and interpreters will detect such an error. Most will not. The gets function reads each character received from the keyboard into an area of memory. The pointer declaration does not set aside memory space for this purpose. If a had been declared a char array, there would have been no problem, assuming that there were enough array elements to contain the keyboard input. However, a pointer should not be used to "hold" anything. (*Note*: A later discussion will explain how pointers can be directed to point to a special area of memory set aside for storage using memory allocation functions. The rules outlined here apply to pointers that have been declared and point to "random" areas of RAM memory.

From this discussion, it should be clear that pointers are special variables that are used specifically to point to certain areas of memory. Actually, all variables—int, double, char, and so on—also point to areas of memory where their assigned values are stored. When any variable is declared, space is set aside to store whatever quantities they are designed to represent. In contrast, a pointer may be thought of as a free agent. Upon declaration, it points to a random area of memory. But a pointer is not tied to a single area of memory, as a common variable is. It can be made to point anywhere. A pointer carries no storage space with it, so it can be used to move all around RAM memory to allow retrieval of previously written data or to allow for data to be written at these locations.

Character pointers can be used to good advantage in many applications, especially when it is desirable to count through each character position. The following program will begin to demonstrate this principle:

```
main()
{

    char *a;

    a = "hello";

    printf("%s\n", a);
    printf("%c\n", *a);

}
```

In this example, a character pointer is declared and points to the beginning of "hello". The first printf line prints the string pointed to by a. The second printf statement prints *a. Again, the unary operator is used, but this time it is not to make a pointer declaration. Notice, also, that the second printf line uses the %c conversion specification, rather than %s, which appears in the preceding line.

When a pointer is used with the unary operator, this indicates that the memory contents (an integer) of one element in the string is to be read. The first printf line will cause the word "hello" to appear on the screen. The next line will display the letter h, the initial character pointed to by *a.

We can take this a step further and actually *count* through each element of the string accessed by the pointer. This is done using the increment operator (+ +). If *a points to the first character in the string "hello", then *a + + counts the pointer to the second element. Another `*a++` counts on to the third element, and so on until the end of the string is reached. The following programs demonstrate this:

```
main()
{

     char *a;
     int x;

     for (x = 0; *a != '\0'; ++x)
          printf("%c\n", *a++);
```

or

```
main()
{

     char *a;
     int x;

     a = "hello";


     while (*a != '\0') {
          printf("%c\n", *a)
          *a++;
     }

}
```

The result of either program is to print

```
h
e
1
1
o
```

on the monitor screen. Each character in the string is accessed individually, displayed, and followed by a linefeed.

It should be understood that `*a++` points to the first character in the string and then counts `*a` by 1. After this operation, `*a` then points to the second character in the string. With each incremental operation, *a points to the next character in the string. This is an exercise in changing the location in memory to which the pointer points.

The following program does the same as the previous two:

```
main ()
{

    char a[6];
    int x;

    strcpy(a, "hello");

    for (x = 0; a[x] != '\0'; ++x)
        printf("%c\n", a[x]);

}
```

All of these programs demonstrate a method whereby each character in a character string may be accessed individually. This is somewhat reminiscent of the MID$ function in BASIC, which can access individual characters or subgroups of characters.

Pointers to character strings in C are actually much easier to use for manipulation of the individual characters than the previous pointer example shown. Instead of using a for loop to display the individual characters, a while loop makes for easier programming:

```
main ()
{

    char *a;

    a = "hello";

    while (*a != '\0')
        printf("%c\n", *a++);

}
```

The while statement portion of this program could also have been written as follows:

```
while (*a != '\0') {
    printf("%c\n", *a);
    *a++;
}
```

The latter version may be a bit easier to understand, as it increments the pointer in a separate statement line. The former example prints the character pointed to and then increments *a in one statement. This is typical of the versatility of C, but such versatility often makes some C constructs difficult for the beginner to understand.

One must be cautious when assigning pointers. The following BASIC program will help set up an example:

```
10 A$="hello"
20 B$=A$
30 PRINT B$
40 A$="goodbye"
50 PRINT B$
```

Here, A$ is assigned an initial value of "hello"; then B$ is assigned a value of A$. Therefore, when line 30 directs the printing of the value of B$, the string "hello" will appear on the screen. Next, A$ is reassigned a value of "goodbye". Again, B$ is printed and it still equals "hello".

In C, we can do the same thing with pointers:

```
main()
{

    char *a, *b;

    a = "hello";
    b = a;
    printf("%s\n", b);
    a = "goodbye";
    printf("%s\n", b);

}
```

Again, the string "hello" will be displayed twice. Now let's try a slightly different approach:

```
main()
{

    char a[20], *b;

    strcpy(a, "hello");

    b = a;

    printf("%s\n", b);

    strcpy(a, "goodbye");

    printf("%s\n", b);

}
```

In this example, only one pointer is used. There is also a char array. The strcpy function is used to copy the constant "hello" into the array. Then pointer b is assigned to a. This means that b will point to the memory location set aside for the array. When b is first used with printf, the string "hello" is found at the location to which it points. Therefore, this string is displayed on the screen. However, another strcpy function is used to change the value of the array to "goodbye". Again, printf is used with pointer b as its argument. This time, the displayed string is "goodbye". The only assignment to b was the memory location of the array. By changing the value of the array (a), we have also changed what b points to. The assignment line of b = a is the same as saying that b will be equal to anything a is equal to.

This did not occur in the initial program, which used two pointers, because a was assigned the memory location of a constant and b was always equal to the constant that appeared at that memory location. When a was later reassigned another constant value, b still pointed to the memory location that held the word "hello". In the second example, strcpy was used to *copy* the contents from one memory location to another, the latter location being that assigned to the char array. The pointer, in turn, was assigned the memory location of the array, *not* that of the constant that was copied to the array. The end result was a pointer that pointed to whatever the array contents were.

Throughout this discussion, I have stressed the fact that a pointer can point to any area of available memory. We have learned that when a pointer points to a character string, it is possible to retrieve each character in the string individually. Since individual characters are stored as integer values in the value range of 0 to 255, we could also display the memory contents of a string as integer values, as in

```
main()
{

    char *a;

    a = "hello";

    while (*a != '\0')
            printf("%d\n", *a++);

}
```

This program will display the ASCII values of the five characters that make up the
word "hello". What has happened here? It may not be obvious, but the pointer has
been used to "peek" into memory and return the values at the location where
"hello" was stored. If a compiler or interpreter is used that allows free access to all
portions of memory (instead of a 64K segment), then pointers may be used to peek
into any area of memory—and to "poke" as well!

To peek or poke into certain areas of memory, it is first necessary to direct a
pointer to the desired area. All past examples of pointer operations have directed
pointers toward areas of memory that were set aside to store constants. We don't
know exactly where these areas are, because the compiler or interpreter simply sets
aside space where it happens to be available. In these operations, it's not necessary
to know the specific locations of this storage space in memory. However, for peek
and poke operations, we must first "aim" the pointer at a specific location.

To direct a pointer to a specific memory location, we simply assign it the
value of that location. It's really quite simple, as the following program will demonstrate:

```
main()
{

    char *a;

    a = (char *) 14500;

    printf("%d\n", *a);

}
```

This is the C equivalent of the following BASIC program:

10 PRINT PEEK(14500)

which assumes a DEF SEG value of 0. In the C program, the pointer is first de-clared, then directed to point to absolute memory location 14500. Most compilers and interpreters will require the cast operator (char *) so as not to confuse the executing environment. Most compliers will generate a warning if the cast operator is omitted, but the program will execute properly. The RUN/C interpreter treats the absence of the cast operator as an error, and execution will halt. Now, a points to memory location 14500. To read the value at this location, we simply print *a. From an earlier discussion, we learned that this will return the value of the first character a points to. The conversion specification in the printf line uses %d, which means that the value read at this location will be displayed as an integer.

Using a pointer directed to a specific location in memory, this program has been able to peek into that memory location. Remember, the memory location must be provided in absolute form. MS-DOS machines divide memory into 64K seg-ments. In BASIC, the DEF SEG statement is used to choose the segment we wish to operate within. For example:

```
10 DEF SEG = &HB800
20 PRINT PEEK(14)
```

Here, DEF SEG specifies the 64K segment beginning at 47104 decimal, or &HB800, and PEEK reads the memory location at byte 14 in this segment. This might lead one to believe that the absolute memory location is 47104 + 14 or 47118. This is totally incorrect, however, because MS-BASIC segment specifications use a truncated form. BASIC adds a 0 to the end of hexadecimal seg-ment specifications to get the absolute address. Adding this zero is the same as mul-tiplying the assigned segment value by 16. So the absolute memory location of &HB800 + 14 is &HB800 * 16 + 14, or &HB8000 + 14. In decimal form, this would be 47104 * 16 + 14, or 753664.

The preceding BASIC program could be written in C as follows:

```
main()
{

    char *a;

    a = (char *) 0xb80001 + 14;

    printf("%d\n", *a);

}
```

It could also have been written as

```
main()
{

    char *a;

    a = (char *) 0xb80001;

    printf("%d\n", *(a + 14));

}
```

The latter representation causes the pointer to point to the fourteenth character or element from 0xb8000. Notice that both programs follow the hexadecimal specification with the letter l. This tells the compiler or interpreter that this constant is a long integer. An uppercase L is also acceptable, but one or the other must follow any long constant. This brings us back to an earlier discussion, where we stated that C likes integers best. If we use values other than integers, we usually must specify that the constant being assigned in other than an integer. In some interpreters or compilers, it is not necessary to specify a long constant when an assignment is being made to a previously declared long variable. However, it's good to get in the habit of following *all* long constant values with an l or L. It can't hurt.

The following program will peek into 1001 successive memory locations, starting at absolute location 0xb8000. This is the start of the graphics screen for IBM Personal Computers and most compatibles:

```
main()
{

    char *a;

    for (a = (char *) 0xb80001; a <= (char *)
    0xb80001 + 1000; ++a)
            printf("%d\n", *a);

}
```

This program uses a simple for loop, which assigns pointer a the memory locations we desire to peek into. On each pass of the loop, the integer value of the character pointed to by a is displayed on the screen. The program could also have been written as follows:

```
main()
{

    char *a;
    int x;

    a = (char *) 0xb80001;

    for (x = 0; x <= 1000; ++x)
        printf("%d\n", *(a + x));

}
```

In the second example, a is initially set up to point to the beginning memory segment. This initial location never changes. However, integer variable x is counted from 0 to 1000 by the for loop. The printf function accesses the memory location of a with an offset of x. This is more like to the method by which a succession of locations are peeked into in BASIC.

We can also poke memory locations using pointers in C. The following program demonstrates this:

```
main()
{

    char *a;

    a = (char *) 14500;

    *a = 255;

}
```

This is the same as the following BASIC program:

```
10  POKE 14500,255
```

assuming that DEF SEG is equal to 0. This is very similar to C language peek operations using pointers, but instead of reading the value pointed to by *a, the value is assigned. Earlier, you were cautioned to remember that pointers contain no memory storage of their own and that assignments to pointers can cause memory locations to be overwritten. This is exactly what is being done with the poke operation. One memory value is being overwritten by another.

The following program will fill the IBM PC graphics screen with solid white by poking each of the 16,385 memory locations with character 255. *Note*: to perform these types of operations using the RUN/C interpreter, you must first use the command SET TRUST ON. This will deactivate the safety feature and allow you to access any area of memory, as follows:

```
main()
{

      char *a;
      int x;

      a = (char *) 0xb80001;

      for (x = 0; x <= 16384; ++x)
            *(a + x) = 255;

}
```

Here, the start of memory is at absolute location 0xb80001. This serves as a reference point throughout the rest of the program. Variable x is counted from 0 to 16384, which marks the beginning and ending offsets of the graphics screen. Within the for loop, the value of x is added to the value of a. A value of 255 overwrites whatever is currently found at the accessed memory location. Note that this program is very similar to the earlier one that read 1001 successive memory locations. Again, for any of these peek or poke operations to work properly with the RUN/C interpreter, the TRUST mode must be set to ON. Make absolutely certain that the programs are input as shown in these pages; don't go poking into random memory locations.

 Most C compilers and interpreters do offer peek() and poke() functions, although they were not a part of the original language. Such functions are still necessary, because the most efficient microcomputer implementations of C on MS-DOS machines restrict memory access to a 64K segment. The peek() and poke() functions allow access to memory outside of this segment. This is usually handled by machine language routines called from C, rather than by functions written in C proper. Nevertheless, the RUN/C peek() and poke() functions could be written as follows, assuming that the TRUST mode is on, giving free access to all memory:

```
peek(x)
long x;
{

      char *a;

      a = (char *) x;

      return(*a);

}
```

```
poke(x, y)
long x;
int y;
{

    char *a;

    a = (char *) x;
    *a = y;

}
```

With the TRUST mode set to ON, these functions would work just like those already contained in the RUN/C function set. It can be seen that pointers and memory access are tied hand in hand. Later in this chapter, you will see how pointers play a roll in memory allocation.

Although only char pointers have been discussed to this point, C also allows the programming of pointers of any type. Therefore, we may have int pointers, float pointers, double pointers, long pointers, and so on. The following program demonstrates the use of an int pointer:

```
main()
{

    int *x, y;

    y = 14;
    x = &y;

    printf("%d\n", *x);

}
```

This program declares x to be an integer pointer (that is, a pointer to a place in memory sized to contain an integer value). A standard int variable, y, is also declared. It is assigned a value of 14. Next, x is directed to point to the memory location set aside for y. We get the memory address of y by preceding this variable with an ampersand (&). After this assignment, x points to the same place in memory that y points to. The next line prints the value in memory that x points to. This will be 14, since this was the value assigned to y.

Here is another demonstration:

```
main()
{

    int *x, y;

    y = 22;
    x = &y;

    printf("%d\n", *x);

    y = 18;

    printf("%d\n", *x);

}
```

This follows the same routine as the last program, but after *x is displayed the first time, the value of y is reassigned. When *x is displayed again, it will be equal to the new value of y. The pointer assignment line, x = &y, means that *x will always be equal to the value of y, regardless of how many times y is assigned or reassigned. Pointer x points to the location in memory that is used to store all assignments made to y. We can do the same thing with other types of pointers, as in

```
main()
{

    double *x, y;

    y = 13.228;
    x = &y;

    printf("%lf\n", *x);

}
```

Here, both the variable and the pointer have been declared double. Therefore, a larger area of memory is set aside to store a double-precision floating point value (64 bits on most MS-DOS implementations). Pointer x will point to the memory location reserved to hold assignments to y, once the proper pointer assignment has been made.

Remember, when a standard numeric variable is preceded by an ampersand (&y), this is a signal to the compiler or interpreter to return or reference the memory location of that variable. The designation &y is a pointer in itself. If discloses the memory location of y. The following program actually lets us see this memory location access:

```
main()
{

    int x;

    x = 14;

    printf("%d\n", &x);

}
```

The printf function argument is &x, or the start of the memory location set aside for integer variable x. Using RUN/C on my IBM Personal Computer, the value of 21754 is displayed on the monitor screen. It may be different on your machine, but in any event, this is the start of the memory location set aside when x was declared. Memory locations will always be integer values, but they are often long integers.

The following programs show another trick:

```
main()
{

    int x;
    x = 22;

    printf("%d\n", peek((long) &x));

}
```

or

```
main()
{

    int x;
    char *a;

    x = 22;
    a = (char *) &x;

    printf("%d\n", *a);

}
```

Both of these programs peek at the contents of memory set aside for holding values assigned to int x. In the first example, the RUN/C peek() function is used. A cast operator coerces the integer memory location of x to a long integer in order to fulfill peek()'s argument requirements. The value returned by peek() will be the same as the value assigned to x, since peek() is reading storage space assigned to x. In the second example, the same thing takes place, except a char pointer is used instead of the peek() function. Here, char *a is made to point to the same memory location assigned to x. Again the value of x is returned.

Note: These programs will return the actual value assigned to x, provided that this value is not more than 255. Either peek routine returns only a single byte from memory, whereas RUN/C uses two bytes to represent integer values. If a value is greater than 255 (the maximum value of a single byte of memory), the second byte is used. For instance, if x = 256, the accessed memory location would be equal to 0 and the next sequential byte would be equal to 1. This is the two-byte code for integer 256.

MEMORY ALLOCATION FUNCTIONS

Closely tied with pointer operations are the memory allocation functions. As has been stated again and again, pointers can be made to point to any area of memory. Typically, pointers are aimed at portions of memory that have already been written to or locations where space has been set aside for storage. But suppose that we want a pointer to point to an area of memory that can be set aside specifically for storage and use the pointer to access this area. Here is where the memory allocation functions come into use. They are especially desirable when it is necessary to set aside a large portion of memory, supposedly to store a lot of data. This could be done by declaring a large char array, but array space is limited, as a certain amount is set aside for this purpose. Once it has been used up, either the space set aside must be enlarged (if possible) or you must resort to another means of storage.

The UNIX memory allocation functions allow areas of memory to be set aside and accessed by a pointer. We don't specify what locations in memory are to be used for this storage, only that we want so many bytes of storage space. These functions attempt to locate such an area that is not currently allocated to some other purpose. When an area or "block" is found, the function allocates the desired number of sequential bytes and returns a pointer to the first byte in this block.

The standard memory allocation functions include malloc() and calloc(). Many compilers designed for microcomputers may have others that are more efficient than these, as they are designed for a particular type of computer or hardware configuration. Generally, however, these specialized functions are not portable, whereas malloc() and calloc() are a part of the standard C language function set and should be supported by every compiler and interpreter.

The malloc() function allocates a block of memory in a way that is compatible with the UNIX operating system. Admittedly, malloc() can be quite inefficient when many small blocks of memory are allocated from a single program, but it provides a universal function on which to base a discussion on memory allocation.

The calloc() function does about the same thing, except that it clears, or sets to 0, each byte in the allocated block. calloc() might be used in place of malloc() if it is necessary to know the length of a string of data that is written to the allocated memory location, with the count stopping at the first cleared byte. Otherwise, the two functions are identical.

The following C program demonstrates the use of malloc():

```
main()
{

    char *a, *malloc();

    a = malloc(800);

    strcpy(a, "Now is the time");

}
```

This example calls malloc() to set aside a block of 800 bytes. A char pointer, a, is assigned the return location from malloc(). This names the location of the first byte in the reserved block.

The next line uses strcpy() to copy the string argument to the memory location pointed to by a. Remember the earlier discussion in this chapter that warned against copying anything to pointers because they do not necessarily point to an area of memory large enough to hold a value, and this could cause a dangerous overwrite of memory currently in use. However, this case is different. Pointer a now has size. It points to an area of memory that contains 800 bytes set aside for access by this pointer only. It is now perfectly safe to copy data to the pointer's location, just as would be done with a declared char array.

This brings up another, more efficient way to program the equivalent of a string array in BASIC. The following program will set up this discussion:

```
10   DIM A$(50)
20   FOR X%=0 TO 50
30   INPUT A$(X%)
40   NEXT X%
```

This example dimensions an array that will hold up to 51 strings. A loop is entered, and on each pass, user input is received from the keyboard and read into each array element. We can accomplish the same thing in C by using a multidimensional char array, but a better way might be to establish an array of char pointers. The following program does just this:

```
main()
{

    int x;
    char *a[51], *malloc();

    for (x = 0; x <= 50; ++x)
        gets(a[x] = malloc(256));

}
```

The declaration char *a[51] sets up an array of char pointers. On each pass of the for loop, gets is used to read the keyboard input. The argument to gets is a[x]. But another operation takes place before data are actually read into a[x]. The location in memory to which a[x] points is returned by malloc(). This function sets aside a maximum storage area of 256 bytes per pointer. This matches BASIC's ability to assign up to 255 characters to a string variable. The extra byte is for the null terminator character. Each pointer is "sized" or directed to a place in memory with adequate storage to hold the input string at the keyboard.

This program duplicates the BASIC example and is the way CBREEZE would handle the translation, but it is a bit wasteful. After all, the input string probably won't be 255 characters in length. The following program demonstrates a more efficient way of doing the same thing:

```
main()
{

    int x;
    char *a[51], b[256];

    for (x = 0; x <= 50; ++x) {
        gets(b);
        a[x] = malloc(strlen(b));
        strcpy(a, b);

    }

}
```

An array of pointers is still declared, but so is a char array of 256 character positions, maximum. The gets function reads its input in the char array; then the pointer is sized using malloc(). The number of bytes malloc() sets aside is determined by the length of the string in b. If the input read to b is 40 characters long, then the pointer is sized to 40 bytes. The contents of b are copied to the pointer's allocated area of memory, which is the exact size to store those contents. Of course, this assumes that

you won't be performing any other operations on the pointer, such as copying another string to the end of what's already there. The pointer is not sized to accept a
larger string.

The following C program demonstrates another use for pointers and memory
allocation functions in C. It sets aside a large block of memory and then writes information to fill the screen. The screen is then saved in this allocated memory block,
a byte at a time. Later, the screen is cleared, but the saved screen still resides in that
block of memory. The last stage of the program restores the erased screen by reading bytes from that block back to the screen memory location:

```
/* BE SURE TO SET TRUST MODE TO ON */

main()
{
        char *a, *b;
        int x;

        a = (char *) 0xb00001;   /* Beginning of video memory */
        b = malloc(4000);

        for (x = 0; x <= 23; ++x)
                printf("Filling screen with data\n");

        for (x = 0; x <= 3999; ++x)
                *(b + x) = *(a + x); /* Read screen bytes to *b bytes */

        cls();

        for (x = 0; x <= 3999; ++x)
                *a++ = *b++;   /* Put bytes from block back on screen */

}
```

This program was written especially for the RUN/C interpreter when used
with the IBM PC monochrome monitor. Note that malloc() is not declared a char
pointer, because this is not legal in RUN/C. This declaration will be mandatory for
most other C environments.

The two char pointers are declared and a is made to point to the beginning of
video memory at 0xb0000. This is a long integer value, and the latter l follows it to
let the environment know that the constant is not an integer. Then malloc() is called
and returns a pointer to a block of 4000 bytes of memory to b. Next, the screen is
filled with a quoted phrase, repeated over and over. When the write is complete,
another loop is entered. This one steps a through 4000 successive memory loca-

tions, comprising the screen. The byte at that screen location is read into b, which is also stepped a byte at a time. When this loop is exited, each of the screen memory bytes has been copied to the memory block.

The screen is now cleared and is supposedly lost forever. However, the next loop performs a reversal of the previous one. During this stage of the program, the contiguous bytes from the allocated block of memory are read into the screen memory. Put simply, the block contains a copy of the original screen, so the block contents are transferred back to screen memory. The end result is the recreated screen display that was present before cls() was executed.

The read and write will take a few minutes because of the slow speed of the interpreter, but the screen is, indeed, captured, stored, and called back when needed. The same thing would have taken place if calloc() had been used instead of malloc(). calloc() accepts a two-part argument in the following format:

```
calloc(number of elements, element length)
```

The first argument is simply multiplied by the second to arrive at the total number of bytes to reserve, but this type of notation allows the second argument to be the sizeof() function, which returns the bytes required for storing various data types. This allows for more portability, since one system may use two bytes to store integers and another may use four. A call such as

```
calloc(100, sizeof(int));
```

sets aside enough memory to store 100 integer values. If a system requires two bytes for each integer, a total of 200 bytes are set aside. But if a program using this line were transferred to a system that used four-byte integers, sizeof() would return a value of 4, and a total of 400 bytes would be reserved. This function is more portable than malloc(), although the latter could be made more portable by expressing it as

```
malloc(100 * sizeof(int));
```

This brings about the same portability.

Of course, there are times when it is desirable to have a whole block of memory containing null bytes (those that have been set to 0). calloc() allocates and clears memory in this fashion. A null block could be used to fill a video screen, thus erasing or clearing it. This might serve in lieu of a cls() function, which is not available in many C implementations.

The C program that saved a screen in a memory block and then called it back after the original screen was cleared performed what is known as a "block move." A block of memory from the video screen location was transferred to another area reserved by malloc(). Technically, the video memory was not moved but was copied from the source location to the destination block. Another block move was performed when the memory from the destination block was copied back to the cleared screen. This was a very slow process when run under an interpreter, and it's still rather slow even when a compiler is used.

Fortunately, a function that was not described as part of the original C language but has become fairly standard in C environments for microcomputers does the same thing. It's called movmem(), and its purpose is to move a block of memory from one location to another. In most implementations, movmem() is written in machine language and is called from C programs. This makes the block transfer as fast as it can be on any particular hardware configuration.

The latest version of RUN/C does contain the movmem() function, and since it is a machine language routine called from the C interpreter, it runs very rapidly. Using this function, the block move described previously, which took several minutes, can now be done in less than a second. The following program uses movmem() to accomplish the same thing our previous example did:

```
/* BE SURE TO SET TRUST ON */

main()
{

        char *a, *b;
        int x;

        a = (char *) 0xb00001; /* Screen address */
        b = malloc(4000);

        for (x = 0; x <= 23; ++x)
                printf("Filling screen with data\n");

        movmem(a, b, 4000); /* Copy screen */

        cls();

        for (x = 0; x <= 200; ++x) /* Time delay */
                ;

        movmem(b, a, 4000); /* Retrieve screen */

}
```

The portion of the program up to the point where the phrases are written to the screen is the same as before. However, the movmem() function is called after the screen is written, and it almost instantly copies the video screen memory to the allocated block. The screen is then cleared. The next loop is a simple time-delay routine. Movmem() works so fast that you might not notice that the screen was cleared before it was written again. This delay loop will accentuate the fact that the screen is cleared. Suddenly, the screen will appear again. It's not slowly written but seems to have been "zapped" back on. In fact, each byte of data is written as before, but because of the machine language nature of movmem(), the write takes place at the fastest possible machine speed.

CLEARING ALLOCATED MEMORY

After a block of memory is allocated and used, it may be desirable to release that block so that it may be reallocated to another pointer or used for some other purpose. It is not efficient to continue allocating block after block of memory when one or two blocks would be sufficient. This would apply when a block is used for a singular purpose and then is no longer needed. The UNIX-compatible memory release function, standard with most C interpreters and compilers, is free(). It is used in the following format:

$$x = free(p)$$

where x is an integer variable and p is a pointer to a previously allocated block of memory. This call will attempt to free the block, making it available for other allocation calls. When free() is called, it returns a code to x. The value of x after the call will be 0 if the release was successful or equal to someother value (usually -1) if there is a release problem. If a problem exists, this is usually a sign of some turmoil within your computer's memory management segment or a sign that the pointer used as an argument to free() does not point to an allocated block of memory.

SUMMARY

Pointers create a lot of confusion for BASIC programmers who are trying to learn C. However, they are nothing more than special variables that can be used to point to anything in memory. Think of a pointer as a *free agent*. When it is initialized, it points to a random location in memory. This might be thought of as pointing to nowhere in particular. But this new type of variable can be assigned the address of something already in memory, giving access to that location at any time. There are pointers to strings, pointers to integers, and pointers to floats. There can even be pointers to pointers.

Pointer operations in C make up a large part of the touted versatility of this language. Because of the unusual nature of pointers, as seen by BASIC programmers, many shy away from delving into this subject. Don't be afraid of pointers. It is true that they are different types of variables from those the BASIC programmer is accustomed to working with. Nevertheless, they should be no stranger than string variables were when you were first learning BASIC.

It should be obvious from this chapter that pointers are closely connected with memory allocation and management. Every computer is different from all others, so the time will come when you will need to use C to program some highly machine-dependent operations. In such cases, it will be necessary to tap your computer's internal architecture. This will certainly require the use of pointers. Once you begin to understand pointers, you will see just how much power and versatility they provide. If you are ever programming again in a BASIC environment, you will miss them.

CHAPTER SIX

BASIC to C Conversion Tables

This chapter contains a major reference source for BASIC programmers who are learning C. The most-used Microsoft BASIC statements and functions are listed alphabetically, along with their C language conversions. In many instances, a special C function has been written to emulate a specific BASIC statement or function for which there is no standard C function. In other instances, standard in-program constructs are used to effect the BASIC operation.

Although many of these conversions are universal and can be ported to many different types of microcomputers, others are highly machine-dependent; they are so noted in the text. All functions and conversions were written in Lattice C, Version 2.15E, and run on an IBM PC. All machine-dependent functions are designed for the IBM PC and 100-percent compatibles.

ABS

BASIC Format:	ABS (arg)
C Format:	abs (arg)
Return Type:	Same as arg

The BASIC ABS function returns the absolute value of its argument. This function directly corresponds to the abs() macro in C. No special translation structure is required. Since abs() is implemented as a macro, it will accept any numeric data type. The type of return is dictated by the argument type. It is usually written in the following manner:

```
#define abs(X)   ((X) < 0) ? -(X) : (X)
```

which means return $-X$ if the value of X is less than 0; otherwise, return X unchanged. In this manner, a positive value of 0 is returned with every argument.

Example

B̲A̲S̲I̲C̲

```
10 X%=ABS(-14)
20 PRINT X%
```

C̲

```
main()
{

    int x;

    x = abs(-14);

    printf("%d\n", x);

}
```

ASC

BASIC Format: ASC (A$)
C Format: asc (a), char *a
Return Type: int

The ASC function in BASIC returns the ASCII code of the first character in its string argument. There is no direct C equivalent of ASC. None is really needed, as any char array value represents each character as its ASCII code. Therefore, a[0] represents the ASCII code of the first character in a. When char pointers are involved, *a represents the first character in a.

The following special function can be used to emulate ASC:

```
asc(s)
char *s;
{

    return((int) *s);

}
```

Most C programs that require return of the ASCII code of the first character in a string value will use the direct method demonstrated within this function, rather than using the function itself.

Example

```
BASIC                          10 A$="HELLO"
                               20 PRINT ASC(A$)


C                              main()
                               {

                                   char *a;

                                   a = "HELLO";

                                   printf("%d\n", *a);

                               }
```

ATN

BASIC Format: ATN (arg)
C Format: atan (arg), double atan (), arg
Return Type: double

The ATN function in BASIC returns the arctangent of a numeric argument. The return value is given in radians. This is equivalent to the atan() function in C. However, ATN accepts any numeric data as its argument. In C, this value must be a double-precision type. Also, atan() must be declared double by every function and/or program that calls it. Again, all arguments to atan() must be double-precision types. This means the use of a double-precision variable or a constant that contains a decimal point and fractional value, even if the fractional portion is zero. Also, the (double) cast operator may be used to coerce other numeric types to double.

Example

```
BASIC                          10 X#=ATN(14)
                               20 PRINT X#


C                              main()
                               {

                                   double x, atan();

                                   x = atan((double) 14);

                                   printf("%lf\n", x);

                               }
```

BEEP

BASIC Format: BEEP
C Format: beep()
Return Type: None

The BEEP statement in BASIC causes an 800 Hz tone to be emitted from the internal speaker for a duration of .25 second. It is the equivalent of PRINT CHR$(7) in the same language. CBREEZE emulates BEEP by using a macro called beep(). It is defined as follows:

```
printf("%c", 7)
```

When beep() is encountered in a C program, the macro definition is substituted.

Example

BASIC   10 BEEP

C   #define beep() printf("%c", 7)
                               main()
                               {

                                   beep();

                               }

BLOAD

BASIC Format: BLOAD FILESPEC, OFFSET
C Format: bload (file spec, offset)
                   char *filespec
                   unsigned offset
Return Type: None

In BASIC, the BLOAD command loads a memory image disk file into a memory location defined by DEF SEG and OFFSET. The OFFSET value is optional. There is no standard C function that can be directly substituted for BLOAD; therefore, it is necessary to write a special one that may be called from a C program. This version requires the offset argument, which is optional in BASIC. It also requires the current offset or segment, which is the equivalent of the DEF SEG value in BASIC. It uses several primitive filekeeping functions to open and read a memory image file written by bsave().

```
bload(a, seg, x)    /* Load a memory file into memory */
|char *a;            /* Name of image file */
int seg, x;         /* seg = DEF SEG value       x = offset */
{
        char *b, *malloc();
        int fil;
        long lseek();
        unsigned n;

        /* Open unbuffered file */

        if ((fil = open(a, 0x8000)) == -1) {
                puts("Cannot open file");
                exit(0);
        }

        n = lseek(fil, 0l, 2);  /* Count bytes in file */
        b = malloc(n);  /* Reserve memory for n bytes */

        lseek(fil, 0l, 0);  /* Return to beginning of file */

        if ((read(fil, b, n)) == -1) {     /* Read bytes to b */
                puts("Cannot read file");
                exit(0);
        }

        _close(fil);      /* Close the opened file */
        poke(seg + x, 0, b, n); /* Poke bytes into memory (Lattice) */

        free(b);    /* Free reserved memory */

}
```

Note: This function is compatible only with files stored using the C function bsave(). It will not properly load files stored by the BSAVE command in BASIC. The Lattice poke() function is used in building this function. When using other compilers/interpreters, some adjustments must be made to address their version of poke().

BSAVE

BASIC Format:	BSAVE filespec, offset, length
C Format:	bsave(filespec, offset, length)
	char *filespec
	int offset
	unsigned length
Return Type:	None

The BSAVE command in BASIC writes memory image data to disk. This statement requires three arguments to specify filename, memory offset, and memory length, respectively.

There is no standard function in C that will perform the same operation as BSAVE, so one must be written. This example, bsave() calls several primitive filekeeping functions that write the sequential bytes in memory to a disk file in a format that can be read and loaded by another special C function, bload(). Both of these special C functions read/write memory image files in formats that are not compatible with BASIC's BLOAD and BSAVE, although the operational results are identical.

```
bsave(a, seg, x, n) /* Save a memory image to disk */
char *a;            /* Name of memory image file */
int seg, x;         /* seg = current DEF SEG value    x = offset */
unsigned n;         /* n = number of bytes to save */
{
        char *b, *malloc();
        int fil;


        /* Create an unbuffered file *\

        if ((fil = creat(a, 0x8000)) == -1) {
            puts("Cannot open file");
            exit(0);
        }

        b = malloc(n);   /* Reserve space to read in bytes */

        peek(x + seg, 0, b, n);  /* Read memory bytes to b */

        if ((write(fil, b, n)) == -1) {    /* Write bytes to disk */
            puts("File write error");
            exit(0);
            }

            close(fil);        /* File is written. Close it */
            free(b);           /* Free reserved memory */

}
```

Note: This function saves memory image information in a format that is not compatible with BASIC's BSAVE. The file must be loaded by the C language bload() function. The Lattice peek() function is used in this example. When this function is written for another compiler or interpreter, it will most likely be necessary to make adjustments for the new environment's equivalent of peek().

CDBL

BASIC Format:	CDBL (X)
C Format:	(double) x
	x may be any numeric type
Return Type:	double

The CDBL function in BASIC converts any numeric data type into a double-precision floating point value. In C, a special operator, (double), does the same thing. This is called a *cast operator* and is identified by the parentheses around it. This operator returns the double-precision value of the numeric expression that follows it.

The term *return* is used loosely in this explanation. In reality, the cast operator behaves much like a separate variable of type double. The expression (x in this example) is assigned to this operator, which results in a double-precision value.

Example

```
BASIC           10 X=14.551
                20 Y#=CDBL(X)


C               main()
                {

                        float x;
                        double y;

                        x = 14.551;
                        y = (double) x;

                }
```

Note: The double cast operator is often used to supply a double-precision value to functions that require this type for arguments, such as the UNIX math functions sqrt(), exp(), cos(), and the like.

CHR$

BASIC Format:	CHR$ (X%)
C Format:	x, int x
Return Type:	None

The CHR$ function returns the character whose ASCII value (0–255) is represented by the value of X%. C is quite versatile, and no special function is required for translation. However, several different translation methods are required, depending upon usage in a program. For example:

```
10 A$=CHR$(65)
```

is best translated via the sprintf function in the following way:

```
sprintf(a$, "%c", 65)
```

The %c conversion specifier instructs the function to assign a$ the character value represented by ASCII 65. This assumes that a$ has been previously declared a char array or initialized pointer.

If CHR$ is used with a PRINT statement to display a character, as in

```
10 PRINT CHR$(65)
```

then the standard printf() function will be used, as follows:

```
printf("%c", 65);
```

In both examples, the *argument* to CHR$ is simply extracted and used to assign a char value, as opposed to a character string value, as is the case in BASIC.

However, if CHR$ should be used in a construct that requires a true string value return, such as

```
10 IF A$=CHR$(65) THEN do something
```

then it becomes necessary to make two tests within the C equivalent of the IF statement line:

```
if (a$[0] == 65 && a$[1] == '\0')
      do something;
```

Here, a check is made to see if the first character in a$ is equal to ASCII 65, and *then* another check is made to see if this is the only character in the string. If both tests prove true, the contents of a$ are indeed equal to the character represented by ASCII 65 and the next line is executed.

It is essential to check for the '\0' string termination character. This means that the string contains only one normal character. This could also be done with the C language strlen() function, as in

```
if (a$[0] == 65 && strlen(a$) == 1)
      do something;
```

Either way, it would be better to calculate the *character* first and forget about comparing an ASCII value with a string. Since ASCII 65 is equal to the letter *A*, it's far simpler to write

```
if (strcmp(a$, "A") == 0)
      do something;
```

Where it is possible, this is the most practical way to translate the original BASIC construct.

CINT

BASIC Format: CINT (X)
C Format: (int) x
                  x may be any numeric type
Return Type: int

The CINT function in BASIC returns an integer equivalent of an argument through a *rounding* operation. Rounding is upward when the fractional portion is equal to 0.5 or more. This also applies to negative numbers, which are rounded toward the next higher negative value when the fractional portion is equal to or greater than -5.

C does not contain a function that will directly replace CINT, and this type of conversion to an integer is a bit foreign to C. Normally, integer conversion is handled by truncating (dropping) the fractional portion of a floating point number. This is equivalent to the method used by the FIX function in BASIC. However, it is quite simple to write a function that will behave exactly like CINT, as the following example demonstrates:

```
cint(x)
double x;
{

     int y, sign;
     double z;

     z = abs(x);             /* z = absolute value of x */
     y = z;                  /* y = x less any fraction */

     if (x < 0)                    /* If x is negative */
          sign = -1;              /* then sign = -1 */
     else                     /* If x is not negative */
          sign = 1;                    /* sign = +1 */

     if ((z - y) >= 0.5)    /* If fraction is .5 or more */
          return((y + 1) * sign);       /* return y + 1 */
     else                         /* If less than .5 */
          return(y * sign);       /* return only y */

}
```

Again, most conversions of floating point values to integers in C are handled by truncating, not by rounding.

CLOSE

BASIC Format: Close #filenum
C Format: fclose (fp)
                   FILE *fp
Return Type: int

The CLOSE statement in BASIC closes a file and frees the filenumber. Running under BASIC, this statement can accept multiple arguments, and each filenumber need not be preceded by the number sign (#). Another usage of CLOSE involves no arguments. This instructs BASIC to close all files that have been opened.

BASIC's CLOSE statement is most equivalent to the standard C function fclose. This function closes a previously opened buffered file, then frees (releases) the file pointer for other use. The FILE pointer itself corresponds to the filenum in BASIC.

The fclose() function does not support using multiple arguments, as CLOSE does, or using no arguments. As is the case in BASIC, C will automatically close all files upon program termination or whenever the exit() function is called.

Example

BASIC   CLOSE #1

C   fclose(fp1);

CLS

BASIC Format: CLS
C Format: cls()
Return Type: None

The CLS statement in BASIC clears the screen, then repositions the cursor at the top left corner. Since this is a machine-dependent operation, there is no standard function in C that can perform the same operation.

It is necessary to write a special function to emulate the CLS operation in C. It addresses the microprocessor's registers and calls an 8086 interrupt. This cls() function in C will properly clear either the monochrome or color screen in the same manner as BASIC's CLS:

```
#include "dcs.h"
cls()    /* Clear screen and set cursor to 0,0 */
{
```

(*continued*)

```
      int attr;
      union REGS r, *inregs, *outregs;

      attr = 0;        /* Color card attribute */
      inregs = &r;
      outregs = &r;

      r.h.ah = 15;     /* "Get current video state" function call (15)
*/

      , int86(0x10, inregs, outregs);   /* Get current state via
interrupt 10h */

      if (r.h.al == 7 !! r.h.al < 4)   /* Check for mono card */
            attr = 7;    /* Monochrome card attribute = 7 */

      r.h.ah = 6;        /* Scroll screen call (6) */
      r.h.bh = attr;     /* Color = 0    Mono = 7 */
      r.h.ch = 0;        /* Upper left corner screen row */
      r.h.cl = 0;        /* Upper left corner screen column */
      r.h.dh = 24;       /* Bottom right corner screen row */
      r.h.dl = 79;       /* Bottom right corner screen column */
      r.h.al = 0;        /* Blank entire window */

      int86(0x10, inregs, outregs);   /* Blank screen by scrolling */

      r.h.ah = 2;        /* Set cursor call (2) */
      r.h.bh = 0;        /* Page number */
      r.h.dh = 0;        /* Row position */
      r.h.dl = 0;        /* Column position */

      int86(0x10, inregs, outregs);   /* Set cursor to 0,0 */

}
```

This function is quite complex, because it was designed to detect the video card in current use (color or monochrome) and then clear the screen with the proper attribute byte (0 for color and 7 for monochrome). However, this entire function can be reduced tremendously if the ANSI.SYS file is made a part of the initial computer configuration upon booting the system. This means writing a file called config.sys. It should contain a single line:

```
      device = ansi.sys
```

With the ANSI device driver installed, the cls() function can be written as follows:

```
      cls()
      {

          printf("\033[2J");

      }
```

Obviously, the ANSI driver makes it very simple to address built-in DOS functions such as CLS and LOCATE and is preferred in most programming environments.

Example

BASIC	10 CLS
C	main()
	{
	cls();
	}

COLOR

BASIC Format:	COLOR foreground, background, border
C Format:	Color (foreground, background)
	int foreground, background
Return Type:	None

The COLOR statement in BASIC sets the foreground, background, and border colors. The following special function emulates the COLOR statement by setting foreground and background colors. The border color is not set by this simple function, but it could easily be included by loading an additional register.

```
#include "dos.h"
color(x, y)      /* Set color background and palette */
int x, y;
{

        union REGS r, *inregs, *outregs;

        inregs = &r;
        outregs = &r;

        r.h.bh = 0;   /* code 0 means set background */
        r.h.bl = x;   /* Background value */
        r.h.ah = 11;  /* "Set color palette" function call(11d) */

        int86(0x10, inregs, outregs);   /* Set background */

        r.h.bh = 1;   /* code 1 means set the palette to be used */
        r.h.bl = y;   /* palette value (0 or 1) */
        r.h.ah = 11;  /* "Set color palette" function call(11d) */

        int86(0x10, inregs, outregs);   /* Set palette */

}
```

This special function uses the Lattice C int86() function to effect an 8086 interrupt.

Example

```
BASIC                          10 COLOR 1,0


C                              main()
                               {

                                   color(1, 0);

                               }
```

cos

BASIC Format:	COS (#X)
C Format:	cos (x)
	double cos(), x
Return Type:	double

The COS function returns the trigonometric functions of angles expressed in radians. The same applies to the cos() function in C; therefore, a direct translation can be made.

However, cos() is a C function that returns a double-precision value, so this function must be declared double at the start of the calling program. This function always requires a double-precision argument. If other types are used, erroneous runs will result. It is up to the user to make sure that all arguments to cos() are doubles. This means using double-precision variables or constant values. The latter must have embedded decimal points.

The CDBL function may be called in order to convert other types of numbers to double-precision in BASIC. The C language cast operator, (double) does the same thing. Some C environments will be able to detect the presence of arguments to cos() that are other than double. However, most will not, so make certain that cos() always receives a double argument. This warning applies equally to other members of the UNIX math set, such as sqrt(), sin(), exp(), tan(), and the like.

Example

```
BASIC                          10 X#=13.889
                               20 PRINT COS(X#)


C                              main()
                               {
```

```
double x, cos();

x = 13.889;

printf("%lf\n", cos(x));

}
```

CSNG

BASIC Format:	CSNG(X)
C Format:	(float) x
	x may be any numeric type
Return Type:	float

The CSNG function returns a value that is a single-precision, floating point equivalent of its argument. This argument may be of any numeric type.

CSNG translates to the (float) cast operator, which coerces its expression to a single-precision type. See CDBL for a further discussion of how cast operators work.

CSRLIN

BASIC Format:	CSRLIN
C Format:	csrlin()
Return Type:	int

The CSRLIN variable returns the line coordinate of the screen cursor. This can be better explained by saying that the line or row position of the cursor is returned as an integer value. There's no standard C function that addresses this operation, as it is highly machine-dependent.

The following is a special function used to emulate this BASIC variable. Various registers are loaded with the needed information, and a DOS interrupt is executed. This function requires no argument.

```
#include "dos.h"
csrlin()     /* Return text cursor line position */
{

    /* This function is identical to pos() except that the value in
dh is returned to  the calling program.   Register dh contains the
current cursor line position */

    union REGS r, *inregs, *outregs;
```

(continued)

```
inregs = &r;
outregs = &r;

r.h.ah = 3;
r.h.bh = 0;

int86(0x10, inregs, outregs);

return((int) r.h.dh + 1);   /* Cursor line position is
                               contained in dl */
}
```

This function calls the Lattice C int86() function, which performs an 8086 interrupt to retrieve the needed register information.

Example

BASIC   10 PRINT CSRLIN

C   main()
                             {

                                 printf("%d\n", csrlin());

                             }

DATE$

BASIC Format:	DATE$ or DATE$ = string
C Format:	date$() or setdate (string)
	char *date$(), *string
Return Type:	char *

In BASIC, DATE$ is a multipurpose variable or statement that sets or retrieves the current date. When used to make assignments, it is a statement used to set the date to the same value indicated by the string argument. The date is always set or returned in the following format:

month:day:year

This is a machine-dependent operation, so there is no standard C function that can be used to get or set the date by accessing the computer's internal clock. In the following discussions, we will translate DATE$ as date$() when the date is being retrieved and as setdate() when the date is being assigned. Both of these are special functions that make DOS function calls. A function to retrieve the system date follows:

```
#include "dos.h"
char *date$()      /* Return system date as a string */
{

        char a[20];
        union REGS r, *inregs, *outregs;

        inregs = &r;
        outregs = &r;

        r.h.ah = 0x2a;  /* "Get date" function call 2ah */

        intdos(inregs, inregs);    /* Get date */

/* The following routine assigns the elements of the system date
to a char array in the same format as BASIC. Register assignments
are: dh = month; dl = day; cx = year */

        if (r.h.dl < 10)
                sprintf(a, "%d-0%d-%d", r.h.dh, r.h.dl, r.x.cx);
        else
                sprintf(a, "%d-%d-%d", r.h.dh, r.h.dl, r.x.cx);

        return(a);     /* Return date as a string */

}
```

DATE$() is declared char * at the beginning of each program or function that calls it, as it will return the date as a string, and in the standard C format described above. If the date is to be set, the special function setdate() is called, with the argument that matches that passed to DATE$ in the BASIC program. In every case, the format of the new date must match that given earlier.

```
#include "dos.h"
setdate(a)    /* Set system date */
char *a;
{
        int m, d, y, x;
        char temp[20];
        union REGS r, *inregs, *outregs;

        strcpy(temp, a);  /* Make temporary copy of argument string */

        x = 0;
        inregs = &r;
        outregs = &r;

        m = atoi(temp);    /* m = month portion of string */

        while (temp[x] != '-')
                temp[x++] = ' ';   /* Move to next numeric sequence */
```

(continued)

```
temp[x] = ' ';
d = atoi(temp);     /* d = day portion of string */

while (temp[x] != '-')
      temp[x++] = ' ';     /* Move to next numeric sequence */
      temp[x] = ' ';
      y = atoi(temp);     /* y = year portion of string */
      y = (y < 1980) ? 1900 + y : y;     /* Correct for abrieviated
date */

/* The following lines assign the extracted date elements to their
proper registers */

      r.h.dh = m;
      r.h.dl = d;
      r.x.cx = y;
      r.h.ah = 0x2b;     /* "Set Date" function call (2bh) */

      intdos(inregs, outregs);     /* Set date */

}
```

The complexity of these functions lies mostly in properly formatting the values that are returned or used to set the clock in a manner that will closely mimic the equivalent BASIC operations.

Example

BASIC

```
10 DATE$="4-5-87"
20 PRINT DATE$
```

C

```
main()
{

    char *date$();

    setdate("4-5-87");

    printf("%s\n", date$());

}
```

DEF FN

BASIC Format:	DEF FName (args) = expression
C Format:	#define fnname (args) expression
Return Type:	Varies

The DEF FN statement in BASIC allows the creation of functions that are written by the programmer. This statement is very similar to the #define macro definition in C. The latter is more versatile, and some highly complex expressions may be used along with various statements. This does not apply to BASIC.

Example

BASIC

```
10  DEF  FNCUBE(X)=X*X*X
20  PRINT  FNCUBE(10)
```

C

```
#define  cube((X))  (X)  *  (X)  *  (X)
main()
{
        printf("%d\n",  cube(10));
}
```

DEF SEG

BASIC Format:	DEF SEG = ADDRESS
C Format:	defseg = address
	int address
Return Type:	None

The DEF SEG statement in BASIC defines the current segment of storage. After a DEF SEG, the use of BLOAD, BSAVE, PEEK, POKE, and the like, will define the actual address as an offset into the segment.

For the Lattice C compiler, DEF SEG is translated into an external integer variable. The assignment of this variable is made within a program that will call any function that defines an offset. An external declaration is made so that each segment address may be used by functions such as peek() and poke() without specifically passing defseg to them. An external variable is known to all functions in a program.

This translation of DEF SEG may not apply to other C environments, many of which require long segment addresses. Segment addressing is common to the MS-DOS machines, but it does not apply to many computers that use other types of microprocessors (the Apple Macintosh, for example). Lattice C requires that the segment and offset addresses for its peek() and poke() functions be given as integer arguments, even though these values are usually long integers. The RUN/C interpreter, on the other hand, requires that the segment and offset be supplied as long integers. There is no standard for peek and poke functions, so many combinations will be found. Again, this discussion involves conversion of BASIC to the small Lattice C compiler.

Example

BASIC
```
10 DEF SEG=100
20 X%=PEEK(14)
```

C
```
int defseg;    /* External variable */
main()
{
        int x;
        char a[2];

        defseg = 100;
peek(defseg, 14, a, 0);

        x = a[0];

}
```

DIM

BASIC Format: DIM var (subscripts), var (subscripts), . . .
C Format: var [subscripts + 1], var [subscripts + 1], . . .
Return Type: None

The DIM statement is used to dimension an array in BASIC; C requires no special statement to size arrays. In making a translation, simply drop the DIM statement and declare array types in the same manner as common variables, with subscripts enclosed in brackets.

BASIC array subscripts name the highest subscript value, whereas C subscript designations name the total number of subscripts. Therefore, the BASIC array

$$DIM \ A\%[20]$$

means that there are 21 array positions, numbered 0 to 20. This assumes an OPTION BASE of 0. In C, the same array would be established as

$$int \ a[21];$$

which means that the integer array may contain 21 total elements. The BASIC and C arrays are identical, but the method of designating subscripts is different.

Arrays of strings are best translated as arrays of char * (string) pointers. The minimum or starting value for an array subscript is 0. On C, there is no equivalent of OPTION BASE, which may be used in BASIC to redefine the minimum subscript value as 1. In C, all arrays are dimensioned with an OPTION BASE of 0 (default).

Example

BASIC   10 DIM A$(10), B%(20), C#(30,40)

C   main()
                          {

                              char *a[11];
                              int b[21];
                              double c[31][41];

                                  etc.

END

BASIC Format:	END
C Format:	exit (0)
Return Type:	None

The END statement terminates program execution after all open files have been closed. The direct equivalent of this statement in C is exit (). This function may be used as a direct substitute for END. The argument value of 0 may be thought of as a dummy value, but other integers may also be used, although their value will have no effect on program termination.

As is the case with BASIC, a C program will close all open files and terminate when the logical program end is reached.

Example

BASIC   10 PRINT "HELLO"
                          20 END

C   main()
                          {

                              printf("hello\n");

                              exit(0);

                          }

EOF

BASIC Format:	EOF (filenum)
C Format:	feof (fp)
	FILE *fp
Return Type:	int

The EOF function in BASIC signals an end-of-file condition by returning a value of −1. If the file end has not been reached, a value of 0 is returned.

EOF may be translated directly into feof(). This is a macro definition that returns a nonzero value (usually −1) when an end of file is detected or 0 when this condition is not true. This macro is handed a FILE pointer as its argument. This pointer is an equivalent to filenum in BASIC.

EXP

BASIC Format:	EXP(X#)
C Format:	exp(x)
	double exp(), x
Return Type:	double

The EXP function returns the mathematical number (e) raised to the X# power. Its direct equivalent in C is exp(), which really is not a standard C function but a member of the UNIX math function set.

Whereas most types of numeric arguments will suffice for EXP in BASIC, C requires the argument to be a double. To provide another type of argument will result in an erroneous return value.

Example

BASIC

```
10 PRINT EXP(10)
```

C

```
main()
{

    double exp();

    printf("%lf\n", exp((double) 10));

}
```

FIX

BASIC Format:	FIX(X)
C Format:	(int) x

x may be any numeric type within the normal integer
range

Return Type: int

The FIX function returns a value that is the integer equivalent of its argument. This
is accomplished by truncating (dropping) any fractional portion of the argument.
Truncation is the method used by C to convert to interger types.

FIX() translates directly to the cast operator (int). See CDBL for a further
discussion of cast operators.

Example

BASIC

```
10 X#=22.889
20 PRINT FIX(X#)
   (Result: 22 is displayed)
```

C

```
main()
{

    double x;

    x = 22.889;

    printf("%d\n", (int) x);

}

   (Result: 22 is displayed)
```

FOR/NEXT

BASIC Format: FOR X = val1 TO val2 STEP val3
C Format: for (x = val1; x ≤ val2; x + = val3) + increment
                  for (x = val1; x −= val2; x -= val3) − increment
Return Type: None

The FOR/NEXT statements form the major looping instruction set in BASIC, although many BASIC programmers would do well to experiment more with the
much less used WHILE/WEND looping mechanism. FOR/NEXT loops translate into
for loops in C. All statements and functions contained in the BASIC loop will also
be a part of the C loop. The loop parameters are established by the arguments to for.

The next C statement will be executed within the loop. When a loop contains
more than one statement, an opening brace ({) must be added to the end of the for

statement line, and all elements are enclosed by it and the closing brace (}), which signals loop termination.

Example

BASIC

```
10   FOR X%=1 TO 20 STEP 1
20   PRINT X%
30   NEXT X%
```

C

```
main()
{

    int x;

    for (x = 0; x <= 20; ++x)
        printf("%d\n", x);

}
```

GOTO

BASIC Format:	GOTO line number
C Format:	goto label:
Return Type:	None

The GOTO statement performs an unconditional branch out of the normal program sequence to another program portion whose access is determined by a specified line number. GOTO is often essential to many types of BASIC programming, but it is the most misused statement in all of BASIC. GOTO branches often cloud comprehension of a program, and the statement is sometimes used as a quick cure for improperly structured programs.

C language will support similar types of branch moves by means of its goto statement, although it is rarely used by good programmers. Whereas GOTO branches to a line number in a BASIC program, goto in C branches to a *label*—a designation composed of letters or letters and numbers, followed by a colon and inserted at the "branch-to" points in the C program. If alphanumeric labels are used, a letter must always start the label name.

Beginning programmers are encouraged *not* to use goto, as almost every C program that uses this statement can be written better without it. Although this statement is fully supported in C, its use is an example of poor programming style. Only in very rare instances can goto be used efficiently. Then why is it available at all? It is available, probably, as a convenience to programmers who may occasionally use it as a means of skipping over large portions of a C program that is being debugged.

The intent here is to discover the bug by skipping around program segments, repair it, and then remove the goto branches. In this usage, goto is a temporary debugging tool.

Example

BASIC

```
10 A$="HELLO"
20 PRINT A$
30 GOTO 20
```

C

```
main()
{

    char a[20];

    strcpy(a, "HELLO");

BD:        /* This is a label */
    printf("%s\n", a);
    goto BD;      /* Goto the Label */

}
```

HEX$

BASIC Format:	A$ = HEX$(X)
C Format:	Varies
Return Type:	None

The HEX$ function in BASIC returns a string that is the hexadecimal equivalent of its integer argument. The return is a string, *not* a hexadecimal number.

In most instances, this function is unnecessary in C language. Any numeric value may be displayed in hexadecimal format (as a number, not a string) by the printf() function. As was the case with CHR$ conversions, all that is necessary is to extract the argument from HEX$ and specify its display in hexadecimal format. A %x conversion specification used with printf() will cause the integer argument to be displayed as a hexidecimal value. If the argument is other than an integer, it must be coerced to an integer using the (int) cast operator. %lx specifies a long hexadecimal integer or one that is larger or smaller than the normal integer range for your computer.

In BASIC, hexadecimal numbers are preceded by &H. In C, the same quantities are preceded by 0x. Thus, &HB800 in BASIC would be 0xb800 in C.

The idea of a HEX$ equivalent in C has never caught on, because it is never necessary. The following demonstrates various translation methods for different BASIC constructs using HEX$.

Example

A$=HEX$(44)   ==   `sprintf(a$, "%x", 44)`

PRINT HEX$(44)   ==   `printf("%x\n", 44);`

A$=B$+HEX$(88)   ==   `sprintf(a$, "%s%x", b$, 88)`

BASIC
```
10 PRINT HEX$(45)
20 X#=45.1
30 PRINT HEX$(X#)
40 PRINT HEX$(47104)
```

C
```
main()
{

    double x = 45.1;

    printf("%x\n", 45);
    printf("%x\n", (int) x);
    printf("%lx\n", 47104L);

}
```

Note: This discussion of HEX$ also applies to OCT$ and CHR$, except for the different values these functions return.

IF-THEN-ELSE

BASIC Format: IF expression THEN clause1 ELSE clause2
C Format: if (expression)
                           clause1
                   else
                           clause2
Return Type: None

The IF-THEN-ELSE statement in BASIC conducts conditional tests based on the true/false value of the expression. If the expression is true, the first clause is executed. If it is false, the second clause is executed. C supports all standard IF-THEN-ELSE constructs, along with the logical operators (AND OR) that are often used as a part of a conditional test. Variations such as ELSE IF and THEN IF are also supported.

Example

BASIC
```
10 X=22
20 IF X=1 THEN PRINT"HELLO" ELSE IF
   X=14 THEN Y=20 ELSE PRINT"GOODBYE"
```

C
```
main()
{
    int x, y;

    x = 22;

    if (x == 1)
        printf("HELLO\n");
    else if (x == 14)
        y = 20;
    else
        printf("Goodbye\n");

}
```

INKEY$

BASIC Format:	A$ = INKEY$
C Format:	a = inkey()
	int a;
	or
	strcpy(a$, inkey$());
	char a$[80], *inkey$()
Return Type:	int or char *

The INKEY$ variable in BASIC reads a single character from the keyboard and returns it as a string. The read is made immediately upon executing INKEY$. If no character is detected in the keyboard buffer, a null character is returned. C offers no function that is equivalent to INKEY$. It is quite simple to write on, however, especially since all that is needed is to test the keyboard for a hit and return the *character* that was typed as a character, not as a string. In BASIC, there is no character data type, only string and numeric types. In C, however, the data type character is all that is needed to emulate INKEY$ adequately. The function follows:

```
inkey()
{
    int hit, c;
```

(continued)

```
hit = kbhit();   /* See if keyboard strike has occurred */

if (hit == 0)    /* If no strike, return -1 */
     return(-1);
else {                  /* If there was a strike */
     c = getch(); /* Get the character */
     return(c);   /* Return the character */
}

}
```

INKEY$ is translated by means of a special C function named inkey(). In examining the code for inkey(), it can be seen that the getch macro is used in conjunction with kbhit() to emulate INKEY$ in BASIC.

The inkey() function first calls kbhit() to see if a keyboard hit has taken place. When one occurs, it immediately calls getch() to retrieve that character and returns as an integer.

If you are a purist and really want a function that behaves exactly like INKEY$ in BASIC—that is, one that returns a keyboard hit as a string, not as another data type—the following modification will do the job:

```
char *inkey$()
{

     char a[2];
     int hit, c;

     hit = kbhit();   /* See if keyboard strike has occurred */

     if (hit == 0)                    /* If no strike, return -1 */
          return(-1);
     else {                           /* If there was a strike */
          a[0] = getch();                  /* Get the character */
          a[1] = '\0'              /* Tack on a NULL character */
          return(a);          /* Return the generated string */
     }

}
```

In this example, the same sequence of events takes place down to the point where getch() enters the execution chain. Here, the retrieved character is assigned to the first character position of char array a[]. Next, a null character (\0) is assigned to the second character position in this array. This makes a character string that consists of the single character returned by getch(). Remember, the addition of the null character allows a character string to be built a single character at a time. Note that the entire function has been declared char * at its beginning. This means that it will return a string pointer, not an integer. Likewise, any program or function that calls inkey$() must also declare it char * before any call is made.

Example

BASIC
```
10 A$=INKEY$
20 IF A$="" THEN 10
30 PRINT A$
```

C
```
main()
{

        int a;

BR10:
        a = inkey();
        if (a == -1)
                goto BR10;

        printf("%c\n", a);

}
```

OR

```
main()
{

        char a[20], inkey$();

BR10:
        strcpy(a, inkey$());
        if (strcmp(a, "") == 0)
                goto BR10;

        printf("%s\n, a);

}
```

The foregoing examples use the much-abused goto statement, which is undesirable from the standpoint of structure. The following program does the same thing as the previous one, but it is written without the goto statement:

```
main()
{

        char a[20], inkey$();
```

(*continued*)

```
strcpy(a, inkey$());
while (strcmp(a, "") == 0)
        strcpy(a, inkey$());

printf("%s\n", a);

}
```

In many instances, while loops may be used to great advantage in avoiding goto in both BASIC and C.

INP

BASIC Format:	INP (P)
C Format:	inp (p)
	int p
Return Type:	int

The INP function returns a single byte from the port named in its argument. In Lattice C, this can be translated directly to inp(). The accessing of ports is a machine-dependent operation; therefore, C offers no standard function to accomplish this operation. However, most modern C compilers and interpreters offer a function to accomplish this, although it may not always be called inp, as it is under the Lattice C compiler. This same discussion applies to outp(), the equivalent of OUT in BASIC. Both of these functions are written in 8086 assembler and called from the Lattice C compiler.

Example

BASIC   10 X%=INP(20)

C   main()
                                   {

                                       int x;

                                       x = inp(20);

                                   }

INPUT

BASIC Format:	INPUT [;]["prompt";] var, var . . .
C Format:	printf ("prompt")
	gets (var) or scanf ("CS", var, var . . .)
Return Type:	None

The INPUT statement in BASIC retrieves formatted input from the keyboard. The actual types of values read depend on the types of variables that serve as arguments to INPUT.

INPUT can be translated in several different ways. First, if a quoted prompt is needed, it is displayed using printf() or puts() on a separate program line, followed by the C input function—gets() or scanf(). (*Note:* puts(a$) is exactly equivalent to printf ("%s\n", a$) and is used for convenience when a single string value is to be displayed and followed by a carriage return.) If the only variable argument to INPUT is a string type, gets() is used. If there are multiple variables to be assigned by the keyboard input, scanf() may be used.

Example

BASIC

```
10 INPUT"Type your name";A$
20 PRINT A$
30 INPUT X%,Y#,Z
40 PRINT X%;Y#;Z
```

C

```
main()
{

    char a[20];
    int x;
    double y;
    float z;

    printf("Type your name\n");
    gets(a);
    puts(a);   /* printf("%s\n", a); */

    scanf("%d,%lf,%f", &x, &y, &z);
    printf("%d %lf %f\n", x, y, z);

}
```

INPUT

BASIC Format:	INPUT #filenum, var, var . . .
C Format:	fgets (var, 80, fp)
	FILE *fp
	char var [80]
	or
	fscanf ("control string", var, var . . .)
Return Type:	char * or int (success indicators only)

INPUT # is a statement that retrieves input from a sequential device such as a file. INPUT # is the file equivalent of INPUT in BASIC, as it retrieves information from a file instead of from the keyboard. The keyboard is also known as the standard input device, whereas the monitor screen is sometimes called the standard output.

In C, the equivalent of INPUT is either gets() or scanf(), depending on what is to be read from the keyboard. As in BASIC, these standard input functions also have file equivalents. They are fgets() and fscanf(). As one might expect, fgets() retrieves a string from an opened file and assigns it to an appropriate pointer. The fscanf() function retrieves numeric data types or a single word (no spaces) from an opened file.

Example

BASIC

```
10 OPEN "TST.FIL" FOR INPUT AS #1
20 INPUT #1, A$
30 PRINT A$
40 INPUT #1,X,Y%,Z#
50 PRINT X;Y%;Z#
60 CLOSE #1
```

C

```
#include "stdio.h"
main()
{
        FILE *fp, *fopen();
        char a[100];
        float x;
        int y;
        double z;

        fp = fopen("TST.FIL", "r");
        fgets(a, 80, fp);
        printf("%s", a);

        fscanf(fp, "%f%d%lf", &x, &y, &z);
        printf("%f %d %lf\n", x, y, z);

        fclose(fp);
}
```

INPUT$

BASIC Format:	X = INPUT$ (N)
C Format:	input$ (x, n)
	char x[80]
	int n
Return Type:	None

The INPUT$ function in BASIC is used to retrieve a string of N characters from the keyboard or the named file. If the keyboard is used for input, the typed characters are not echoed to the screen.

There is no standard C function that can accomplish this operation, so one must be written. In this example, INPUT$ is supported only as it is used to retrieve information from the keyboard, not from a named file. This function uses a *for* loop to execute a getch() function during each cycle. The loop cycles the number of times specified by N(n). The getch() function reads a single character from the keyboard. On each pass of the loop, the input character is assigned to a char array.

```
input$(a, n)    /* Assign n characters from the keyboard to a */
char a[];
int n;
{
    int x;

    for (x = 0; x < n; ++x)   /* Count from 0 to n - 1 characters */
        a[x] = getch();       /* Get a single character from keyboard */

    a[n] = '\0';    /* Terminate string with NULL character */

}
```

This function duplicates the operation of the BASIC INPUT$ statement when it is used to retrieve information from the standard input (keyboard).

Example

```
BASIC               10 A$=INPUT$(10)
                    20 PRINT A$

C                   main()
                    {

                        char a[11];

                        input$(a, 10);
                        printf("%s\n", a);

                    }
```

INSTR

BASIC Format:	X% = INSTR(A$,B$)
C Format:	x = instr(a$, b$)
	int x
	char a[80], b[80]
Return Type:	int

The INSTR function searches for the first occurrence of B$ in A$ and returns the character position at which the match is found.

In C, a special function is needed to emulate INSTR. A loop is set up in the special function that counts through the characters in a$, comparing them with those in b$. If a match is found, the loop is exited and the character position (+ 1) of the match is returned. In C language, character counts always begin with position 0. INSTR begins its count at 1. Therefore, it is necessary to increment a match position calculated by the C function in order to emulate the BASIC function accurately.

```
instr(a, b)     /* Find occurrence of b in a */
char a[], b[];
{

    int x, y, z;

    for (x = 0; a[x] != 'O'; x++) {  /* Count through a */
        for (y = x, z = 0; b[z] != 'O' && a[y] == b[z]; y++, z++)
            ;    /* Seek match */

        if (b[z] == '\0')   /* Match found--return index */
            return(x + 1);
    }

    return(0);   /* No match is found--return 0 */

}
```

In BASIC, INSTR may also be supplied with an integer argument that specifies where the search is to begin. This example does not support this operation, but it could easily be included by supplying the x loop variable with a starting value that is determined by a third argument that could be passed to the function, instead of 0, as shown.

Example

BASIC
```
10 A$="NOW IS THE TIME"
20 B$="THE"
30 PRINT INSTR(A$,B$)
```

C
```
main()
{

    char *a, *b;

    a = "NOW IS THE TIME";
    b = "THE";

    printf("%d\n", instr(a, b);

}
```

INT

BASIC Format:	INT(X)
C Format:	floor((double) x)
	x is any numeric type
Return Type:	int

The BASIC INT function returns the integer equivalent of its argument.

In C, conversion to integers is normally accomplished using the truncation method. This is the way the FIX function returns an integer in BASIC. The INT function truncates all positive integers, as FIX does, but negative integers are rounded upward in a negative direction. However, it is possible to exactly duplicate the INT function in BASIC by means of the following C function:

```
bint(x)
double x;
{

    int y;

    y = x;                      /* y = truncated integer value of x */
    if (x >= 0 || (x - y) == 0)    /* if x is pos. or has no fract */
        return(y);              /* return the value of y */
    else                        /* if x is negative with a fraction */
        return(y - 1);          /* add -1 to y */

}
```

Note: This function is presented for discussion purposes only. In most situations, the cast operator (int) will be all that is required for conversion to integers. Only in special situations will the truncation of positive numbers and the rounding of negative numbers be desirable, and a function similar to the one above may be called upon.

There is another answer as well. Lattice C and many other C environments offer a function from the UNIX math function set called floor(). This function accepts a double argument and returns a whole number that lies just below each argument value. This return is a double, but it is a whole number with a fractional component of 0. Therefore, all that is necessary to convert this return to an integer is the (int) cast operator. Even easier, simply assign the return from floor() to an integer variable, as follows:

```
int x;
x = floor(33.7);
x = -33.7;
```

The floor() function always returns a whole number that lies below the total value or the value itself when the fractional component is 0. In the foregoing example, x is first equal to +33 and then to −34. These are the whole values that lie just below the argument values. Remember, floor() requires a double argument and returns a double value. Therefore, this function must be declared double by any program that calls it.

KILL

BASIC Format:	KILL"filespec"
C Format:	unlink ("filespec";)
	char *filespec
Return Type:	None

The KILL command in BASIC deletes a disk file. In C, simply translate this command to the primitive file function called unlink().

Example

> **BASIC**   **KILL"TST.FIL"**

> **C**   **unlink("TST.fil");**

LEFT$

BASIC Format:	A$ = LEFT$(B$,N)
C Format:	left$(a$, b$, n)
	char a[80], b[80]
	int n
Return Type:	None

The LEFT$ function returns the leftmost characters in B$ up to a total of N characters. If the entire string is composed of fewer than N characters, the entire string is returned.

There is no standard function in C that can be used to replace LEFT$, so it is necessary to write one. It is important to note that LEFT$ in BASIC and the other substring functions, such as RIGHT$ and MID$, actually return a value. Although string pointers can be returned in C, this can add to the confusion experienced by learning programmers. This discussion centers around a left$() function that is more in line with similar standard C functions. It is designed to write the specified substring from one of its argument strings to another argument string. It does not return any usable value but assigns a substring to a supplied char pointer or char array that is also a part of its argument complement. For this reason, it is suggested that you direct translation of BASIC program lines such as the following:

> **PRINT LEFT$(B$, 5)**

This requires a return value to PRINT rather than to some other variable, such as B$. When translating substring functions to C, it is best to start with a BASIC program such as

```
30 A$=LEFT$(B$,5)
40 PRINT B$
```

This program segment accomplishes exactly what the one before it did, but separate operations are used for assignment and for display.

The C function left$() does not return any value. Instead, it sends a copy of the leftmost characters in a target string to a character array that is one of its arguments:

```
left$(a, b, x)     /* Return leftmost characters in b to a */
char *a, *b;
int x;
{
        int i;

        i = 0;

        while (i++ < x)    /* Count from zero to x - 1 characters */
             *a++ = *b++;    /* a = specified substring */

        *a = '\0';     /* Terminate a with NULL character */

}
```

Note that this function accepts the string pointer that contains the substring (b) and the pointer to which the substring is to be assigned (a) as its arguments in addition to x, which names the number of leftmost characters. After this function is executed, a will be equal to the specified substring in b. This function returns no usable value; therefore, it cannot be used as an argument to other functions, such as printf().

Example

BASIC
```
10 B$="COMPUTER"
20 A$=LEFT$(B$,3)
30 PRINT A$
40 REM This program displays "COM"
```

C
```
main()
{

        char a[20], b[20];

        strcpy(b, "COMPUTER");
        left$(a, b, 3);
```

(continued)

```
                    printf("%s\n", a);

                    /* This program displays "COM" */

       }
```

LEN

BASIC Format:	X% = LEN(A$)
C Format:	x = strlen (a$)
	int x
	char a$[80]
Return Type:	int

The LEN function returns the number of characters in a string argument. Fortunately, there is a C function called strlen() that will do the same thing. It is a direct substitution that can be made whenever LEN is encountered.

This function returns the total number of characters in a C string, except for the null terminating character (\0). Therefore,

10 X%=LEN("COMPUTER")

in BASIC, and

x = strlen("COMPUTER");

in C will both return a value of 8.

LINE INPUT

This statement is the same as INPUT when translated to C. See INPUT for a full discussion.

LOCATE

BASIC Format:	LOCATE row,col,cursor,start,stop
C Format:	locate (row, col)
	int row, col
Return Type:	None

The LOCATE statement in BASIC positions the cursor on the display screen and, optionally, turns the cursor on or off. It may be used to determine cursor size as well.

Any routine that positions the cursor on the screen will be machine-dependent. Since there is no standard function in C that will permit this operation, it is necessary to write a special function that will access the IBM PC interrupts. One example follows:

```
#include "dos.h"
locate(x, y)      /* Place text cursor at coordinates x, y */
int x, y;
{

        union REGS r, *inregs, *outregs;

        inregs = &r;
        outregs = &r;

        r.h.ah = 2;     /* "Set cursor position" video call(2) */
        r.h.bh = 0;     /* Page number */
        r.h.dh = x + 1;     /* dh register = x + 1 */
        r.h.dl = y + 1;     /* dl register = y + 1 */

        int86(0x10, inregs, outregs);     /* Set cursor via interrupt
                                             10h */


}
```

This function uses the int86() function common to Lattice C and several other compilers and interpreters to make an 8086 interrupt. Various registers are read that set the current cursor position.

As was the case with CLS, if the ANSI driver is installed upon booting the computer, a far easier method of setting the cursor may be had. Refer to CLS for more information on the ANSI driver. The following ANSI function will place the cursor at the desired screen position:

```
locate(x, y)
int x, y;
{

        if (x < 1 || x > 25 || y < 1 || y > 80)
            return;
        else
            printf("\033[%d;%dH", x, y);

}
```

This is far simpler than the non-ANSI example that preceded it.

Example

```
BASIC              10 LOCATE 10,10


C                  main()
                   {

                       locate(10, 10);

                   }
```

LOG

BASIC Format:	LOG(X#)
C Format:	log(x)
	double log(), x
Return Type:	double

The LOG function returns the natural logarithm of its argument. In BASIC, the argument may be any numeric type. The direct equivalent of BASIC's LOG function is the UNIX math function log().

In C, log() must be declared double at the start of any program or function that calls it, and all arguments to log() must also be doubles. To provide another type of argument will result in a bad return value.

Example

```
BASIC              10 PRINT LOG(14)


C                  main()
                   {

                       double log();

                       printf("%lf\n", log((double) 14));

                   }
```

LPRINT

BASIC Format:	LPRINT args[;]
C Format:	fprintf (fp, "cs", args)
	FILE *fp (= LPT1:)
Return Type:	int

The LPRINT statement in BASIC is the same as PRINT except that all output is directed to the parallel printer rather than to the monitor screen.

In C, it is necessary to open the printer port as you would a file and write to this device using fprintf(), fputs(), or any other functions that are file equivalents of functions that normally write to the standard output (printf, puts, putchar, etc.). The FILE functions simply redirect output from the standard output to the named device or file.

The Lattice C compiler allows the parallel printer port of the IBM PC to be opened as LPT1: or LPT2:, depending on which port is driving the printer.

Example

B̲A̲S̲I̲C̲   10 LPRINT"HELLO"

C̲   #include "stdio.h"
                              main()
                              {

                                     FILE *fp, *fopen();

                                     fp = fopen("LPT1:", "w")

                                     fprintf("HELLO\n");

                                     fclose(fp);

                              }

MID$ (Function)

BASIC Format: A$ = MID$ (B$,START,N)
C Format: mid$(a$, b$, start, n)
                    char a$[80], b$[80]
                    int start, end
Return Type: None

The MID$ function returns a portion of a given string that is defined by the starting character position and the character count arguments (START and N).

No standard C function can be directly substituted for MID$, so one must be written. The following special function behaves similarly to the left$() function discussed earlier. Review the discussion of that function to be aware of the restrictions applied to the substring functions and how they differ from their BASIC counterparts.

The source code for mid$() follows:

```
mid$(a, b, x, y)    /* Return specified substring */
char *a, *b;
int x, y;
{

    --x;    /* Starting substring character position */
    y += x;   /* Ending substring character position */

    while (x < y && x <= strlen(b))  /* Count through substring */
        *a++ = *(b + x++);    /* a = specified substring */

    *a = '\0';    /* Terminate a with NULL character */

}
```

As was the case with left$(), this function requires that the char array variable that is to represent the extracted substring be included as part of the argument complement to mid$(). This function does not *return* any usable value but writes the substring to the memory location provided by a.

Example

BASIC

```
10 B$="COMPUTER"
20 A$=MID$(B$,4,3)
30 PRINT A$
```

C

```
main()
{

    char a[20], b[20];

    strcpy(b, "COMPUTER");

    mid$(a, b, 4, 3);

    printf("%s\n", a);

}
```

MID$ (Statement)

BASIC Format:	MID$(A$,START,N) = B$
C Format:	mids$(a$, start, n, b$)
	char a$[80], b$[80]
	int start, n
Return Type:	None

The MID$ statement places one argument string within another, based on two character position values. The contents of the assigned string are substituted for the character portion identified by the values of START and N.

A special C function must be written to emulate these operations. The mids() function accepts two character array arguments plus the starting character position and the character count. The value of the last string is placed at the proper position within the first.

Remember, we are discussing the MID$ *statement* here; the MID$ function was discussed previously. The function returns a substring from a string, whereas the statement writes a substring into a string. The source code for mids() follows:

```
mids(a, x, y, b)     /* Place b in a as substring */
int x, y;
char *a, *b;
{

    int l;

    l = strlen(a) - 1;
    y += x;     /* Starting substring character position */
    --x;

    while (x <= y && x <= l && *b != '\0')
        *(a + x++) = *b++;     /* Replace characters in a with b */

}
```

This C function will effectively write the string pointed to by b into the one pointed to by a and at the character positions starting at x and ending at y.

Example

BASIC

```
10 B$="PUT"
20 A$="COMXXXTER"
30 MID$(A$,4,3)=B$
40 PRINT A$
50 REM DISPLAYS "COMPUTER"
```

C

```
main()
{

    char a[20], b[20];

    strcpy(b, "PUT");
    strcpy(a, "COMXXXTER");
```

(continued)

```
mids(a, b, 4, 3);

printf("%s\n", a);

/* Displays "COMPUTER" */

}
```

OCT$

BASIC Format:	OCT$(X%)
C Format:	Varies
Return Type:	Octal integer

The OCT$ function returns a string that is an octal equivalent of the decimal argument, X%.

No special function is needed to convert a numeric quantity to its octal equivalent in C. The main purpose for this type of conversion is for display, and the printf() function will display any integer quantity in octal format when the %o conversion specification is used (%lo for long integer conversions). In C, octal quantities are identified by the leading 0. Therefore, the octal value 377 would be written in a C program as 0377.

The idea of an OCT$ equivalent in C has never caught on, because it is never necessary. The following demonstrates various translation methods for different BASIC constructs using OCT$.

Example

```
A$=OCT$(27)             ==              sprintf(a$, "%o", 44)

PRINT OCT$(27)          ==              printf("%o\n", 44);

A$=B$+OCT$(27)          ==              sprintf(a$, "%s%o", b$, 88)
```

```
    BASIC               10 PRINT OCT$(32)
                        20 X#=35.6
                        30 PRINT OCT$(X#)
                        40 PRINT OCT$(46890)


    C                   main()
                        {

                            double x;
```

```
                                   printf("%o\n", 32);
                                   printf("%o\n", (int) x);
                                   printf("%o\n", 46890L);


                    }
```

Note: This discussion of OCT$ also applies to HEX$ and CHR$, except for the different values these functions return.

OPEN

BASIC Format:	OPEN filespec FOR mode as #filenum
C Format:	fp#filenum = fopen (filespec, "mode")
	FILE *fpfilenum, *fopen()
Return Type:	FILE pointer

The OPEN statement in BASIC opens a file or device. Arguments name the file to be opened, its mode, and the filenumber.

In C translations, OPEN is converted to the fopen() function. The file operation is either r, w, or a, for read, write, or append. The filenumber is converted to a FILE pointer. This is the original number found in the BASIC program, preceded by fp.

It is necessary to #include the header file "stdio.h" in every translation that calls a file function. This header file contains the definitions and structures needed for any filekeeping operations.

Example

BASIC

```
                    10 OPEN "TST1.FIL" FOR INPUT AS #1
                    20 OPEN "TST2.FIL" FOR OUTPUT AS #2
                    30 OPEN "TST3.FIL" FOR APPEND AS #3
```

C

```
                    #include "stdio.h"
                    main()
                    {

                        FILE *fp1, *fp2, *fp3, *fopen();

                        fp1 = fopen("TST1.FIL", "r");
                        fp2 = fopen("TST2.FIL", "w");
                        fp3 = fopen("TST3.FIL", "a");


                    }
```

OUT

BASIC Format:	OUT P%,N%
C Format:	out(p, n)
	int p, n
Return Type:	None

The OUT statement sends a byte to a machine output port. Most microcomputer implementations of C offer an equivalent of OUT as a machine-dependent function (named outp() in Lattice C).

When using the Lattice C compiler, you may translate OUT directly to outp(). Although the original C language did not contain it as a part of the standard function set, outp() is almost universally found in C environments for most microcomputers. It is often a machine language function that is called from C.

Example

BASIC   10 OUT 980,2

C   main()
                             {

                                  outp(980, 2);

                             }

PEEK

BASIC Format: PEEK (X)
C Format: peek (seg, offset, a, byte)
                 int seg, offset;
                 char *a;
                 unsigned byte;
Return Type: int

The PEEK function returns a byte from a memory offset defined by X. Any DEF SEG value that is in effect at the time PEEK is called defines the current segment.

The standard C function set has no peek function, since it is not necessary in implementations that address all memory locations directly. However, the IBM PC and compatible machines use processors that section off memory into 64K segments. This creates difficulties where standard C implementations are used. Through 2-byte pointers, it is possible to directly address a location within the segment but not outside it. Recently, compilers have been modified to offer several different implementations or memory models. The large-memory models use four-byte pointers to address all memory, but these models are not as efficient as the small-memory versions that allow only a 64K address.

However, special functions have been developed for small-memory models of most compilers to allow all of memory to be accessed by peek() and poke() functions. How these functions are implemented varies from compiler to compiler. In Lattice C, both require a segment and an offset argument, which must be specified as integers or assigned to integer variables, even if their values place them in the long int category. The return value (for peek) or the value to be placed in memory (for poke) is assigned to a char array or string pointer. The following assumes use of the small-model compilers.

Example

BASIC   10 DEF SEG=100
                               20 X%=PEEK(25)

C   main()
                               {

                                   int x;
                                   char a[2];
                               peek(100, 25 a, 1);

                               x = a[0];

                               }

If a large-model compiler is being used, the following function will correspond to peek():

```
peek(x)   /* x = DEF SEG times 16 + offset */
long x;
{

    char *a;

    a = (char *) x;

    return((int) *a);

}
```

POINT

BASIC Format: POINT(X%, Y%)
C Format: point(x, y)
                 int x, y
Return Type: int

POINT is the only graphics function common to MS-BASIC—or, more accurately, to PC- or GW-BASIC. It returns the color value or index of a pixel located at the coordinates specified by X%, Y%.

Since any graphics operation is machine-dependent, the standard C function set contains no such function. The following is a special function called point(), which can be used to read the color index of the pixel. This is accomplished by making a DOS function call. The color value is returned as an integer.

```
#include "dos.h"
point(x, y)    /* Read pixel color index at coordinates x, y */
int x, y;
{

    union REGS r, *inregs, *outregs;

    inregs = &r;
    outregs = &r;

    r.x.cx = x;     /* cx = x-coordinate */
    r.x.dx = y;     /* dx = y-coordinate */
    r.h.ah = 13;    /* "Read dot" function call(13d) */

    int86(0x10, inregs, outregs);    /* Read pixel color */

    return((int) r.h.al);    /* Return color value */

}
```

This is a simple function that makes a DOS function call to read the color index at the specified screen coordinates.

Example

BASIC   10 X%=POINT(160,100)

C   main()
                                   {

                                       int x;

                                       x = point(160, 100);

                                   }

POKE

BASIC Format: POKE X%,Y%
C Format: poke (seg, offset, a, byte)

                                int seg, offset;
                                char *a;
                                unsigned byte;
    Return Type: None

The POKE statement in BASIC writes a byte to a memory location. The Lattice C compiler contains its own poke() function, but like the peek() function, it requires pointer operations. This makes it difficult to make a direct translation.

The standard C function set has no poke function, since it is not necessary in implementations that address all memory locations directly. However, the IBM PC and compatible machines use processors that section off memory into 64K segments. This creates difficulties where standard C implementations are used. Through two-byte pointers, it is possible to directly address a location within the segment but not outside it. Recently, compilers have been modified to offer several different implementations or memory models. The large-memory models use four-byte pointers to address all memory, but these models are not as efficient as the small-memory versions that allow only a 64K address.

However, special functions have been developed for small-memory models of most compilers to allow all of memory to be accessed by peek() and poke() functions. How these functions are implemented varies from compiler to compiler. In Lattice C, both require a segment and an offset argument, which must be specified as integers or assigned to integer variables, even if their values place them in the long int category. The return value (for peek) or the value to be placed in memory (for poke) is assigned to a char array or string pointer. The following assumes use of the small-model compilers.

Example

```
BASIC                    10 DEF SEG=1000
                         30 POKE 10,255


C                        main()
                         {
                              char a[2];

                              a[0] = 255;
                              a[1] = '\0';

                              poke(1000, 10, a, 1);

                         }
```

If a large-model compiler is used, poke() may be generally defined as follows:

```
poke(x, y)
long x;   /* x = DEF SEG times 16 + offset */
int y;
{

     char *a;

     a = (char *) x;   /* Set location */
     *a = y;           /* Write byte to location */

}
```

POS

BASIC Format: POS(X%)
C Format: pos()
Return Type: int

The POS function in BASIC returns the current cursor column position. The argument value is unimportant, since this is a dummy argument.

There is no function in C that will emulate this machine-dependent BASIC function, but one can be written easily. The same 8086 interrupt is called as for the CSRLIN variable, but a different register is read to retrieve the column position instead of the row position.

```
#include "dos.h"
pos()     /* Return text cursor column position */
{

     union REGS r, *inregs, *outregs;

     inregs = &r;
     outregs = &r;

     r.h.ah = 3;   /* "Read cursor position" video call(3) */
     r.h.bh = 0;   /* Page number */

     int86(0x10, inregs, outregs);   /* Get position via interrupt
                                        10h */

     return((int) r.h.dl + 1);   /* Return column position in dl */
```

Note that this function requires no argument.

Example

BASIC   10 PRINT POS(0)

C   main()
                                {

                                        printf("%d\n", pos());

                                }

PRINT

BASIC Format: PRINT ARG; ARG; ARG; . . .
C Format: printf ("control string", arg, arg, arg, . . .)
Return Type: None

The PRINT statement in BASIC is used to write formatted output to the screen. In
C, printf() is the function used for the same purpose. Unlike PRINT, printf() requires
that a control string precede any arguments to indicate the types of arguments to be
expected and the exact format of their display.

Example

BASIC   10 PRINT"HELLO"
                        20 A$="GOODBYE"
                        30 B$="COMPUTER"
                        40 PRINT A$;B$
                        50 PRINT A$, B$
                        60 X%=1
                        70 Y%=12
                        80 PRINT X%;Y%
                        90 S#=46.886
                        100 T#=112.712
                        110 PRINT T#;X%;A$;S#;"LANGUAGE"

C   main()
                        {

                                char *a, *b;
                                int x, y;
                                double s, t;

                                printf("HELLO\n");

                                a = "GOODBYE";
                                b = "COMPUTER";

                                                        (*continued*)

```
printf("%s%s\n", a, b);
printf("%s%-14s\n", a, b);

x = 1;
y = 12

printf(" %d    %d\n", x, y);

s = 46.886;
t = 112.712;

printf(" %lf    %d %s %lf %\n", t, x,
a, s, "LANGUAGE");
```

}

PSET

BASIC Format:	PSET (X%,Y%), C
C Format:	pset (x, y, c)
	int x, y, c
Return Type:	None

The PSET statement sets a point on the graphics screen at the coordinates specified
by X%,Y% and in a color index of C.

There is no standard C function that will serve as a direct substitute for PSET,
so the following special function was written:

```
#include "dos.h"
pset(x, y, c)    /* Set a pixel at x, y in color c */
int x, y, c;
{

    union REGS r, *inregs, *outregs;

    inregs = &r;
    outregs = &r;

    r.x.cx = x;    /* cx = x-coordinate */
    r.x.dx = y;    /* dx = y-coordinate */
    r.h.al = c;    /* al = color index */
    r.h.ah = 12;   /* "Write dot" function call (12d) */

    int86(0x10, inregs, outregs);   /* Set pixel */

}
```

This function works exactly like PSET in BASIC by making a DOS function call.

This function might be thought of as the opposite of point(), which was discussed earlier.

Example

```
BASIC                    10 PSET(160,100),2


C                        main()
                         {

                             pset(160, 100, 2);
```

RANDOMIZE   `}`

BASIC Format:	RANDOMIZE X
C Format:	srand ((long) x)
	x may be any numeric type within the normal integer range
Return Type:	None

The RANDOMIZE statement reseeds the random numbers generator and may be used with a numeric argument, although this is optional in BASIC. Without an argument, RANDOMIZE causes execution to halt, and a prompt is displayed asking for an input value. For translation into C, however, this statement must have an argument.

Various C programming environments for microcomputers use different functions for generating a random number. In this example, we will convert RANDOMIZE to srand48(), a Lattice C function. This one requires a long integer argument, so the (long) cast operator is used to coerce the argument supplied in the BASIC program to a long integer value that is compatible with the function. Longs are not directly supported by BASIC.

After reseeding has taken place, calls to the drand48() function, the equivalent of RND in BASIC, will return refreshed random numbers. See RND discussion.

Example

```
BASIC                    10 RANDOMIZE 14


C                        main()
                         {

                             srand48((long) 14);

                         }
```

REM

BASIC Format: REM remark
C Format: /* remark */
Return Type: None

The REM statement allows comments to be embedded in BASIC programs. REM
statements are not executed. They only serve to explain various program sections
through comment lines.

All REM statements may be translated into C program comment lines that begin with /* and end with */. All comments are nested between the two delimiters.

Example

BASIC

```
10 PRINT"HELLO"
20 REM THE ABOVE LINE DISPLAYS "HELLO"
```

C

```
main()
{

        printf("HELLO\n");

        /* THE ABOVE LINE DISPLAYS "HELLO"

}
```

RIGHT$

BASIC Format: A$ = RIGHT$(B$,N)
C Format: right$(a$, b$, n)
                   char a$[80], b$[80]
                   int n
Return Type: None

The RIGHT$ function returns the rightmost N characters in the string argument.

As was the case with LEFT$ and MID$, a special function must be written to
emulate in C the operations of RIGHT$. Refer to LEFT$ for a discussion of the limi-
tations of the various substring functions. The C version of RIGHT$ may be ob-
tained with the following function:

```
right$(a, b, x)      /* Return rightmost characters in b to a */
char *a, *b;
int x;
{

        int i;
```

```
x = (x > strlen(b)) ? strlen(b) : x;
i = strlen(b) - x;   /* i = starting character in string */

while (i < strlen(b))   /* Count from start to string end */
      *a++ = *(b + i++);   /* a = specified substring */

*a = '\0';       /* Terminate string with NULL character */
}
```

This function does not return a usable value but writes the substring at the memory location pointed to by a.

Example

BASIC

```
10 B$="COMPUTER"
20 A$=RIGHT$(B$,3)
30 PRINT A$
40 REM DISPLAYS "TER"
```

C

```
main()
{
    char a[20], b[20];

    strcpy(b, "COMPUTER");
    right$(a, b, 3);

    printf("%s\n", a);

    /* DISPLAYS "TER" */
}
```

RND

BASIC Format:	X = RND
C Format:	x = drand48()
	double drand48(), x
Return Type:	double

The RND function returns a random number between 0 and 1. This function is most often used as a constantly changing variable, in that RND is equal to a random value each time it is called.

In Lattice, RND can be translated as drand48(). This function is declared double at the beginning of any program or function that calls it and always returns double values between 0 and 1.

Example

BASIC   10 X#=RND

C   main()
                               {

                                   double x, drand48();

                                   x = drand48();

                               }

SCREEN (Statement)

BASIC Format: SCREEN mode,burst,apage,vpage
C Format: screen(mode, burst)
                   int mode, burst
Return Type: None

The SCREEN statement in BASIC sets the screen attributes to be used by other statements that write information to the screen.

You must write a special C function when translating the BASIC SCREEN statement. The operations performed by this statement are machine-dependent and are not emulated by any of the functions in the standard C language set.

The following C function supports only mode and burst arguments to screen(), although the active and visual page determination could also be accomplished through a more complex function.

```
#include "dos.h"
screen(mode, burst)       /* Set screen mode -- Color Graphics Card */
int mode, burst;
{

    union REGS r, *inregs, *outregs;

    inregs = &r;
    outregs = &r;
    burst = burst % 2;   /* Make sure burst = 0 or 1 */
    r.h.ah = 15;    /* "Get mode" function call (15d) */

    int86(0x10, inregs, outregs);    /* Get current screen mode */
```

```
/* The following routine assigns a new mode/burst value based upon
the current value and the one desired */
        if (mode == 0 && r.h.ah > 40)
                mode = 2 + burst;
        else if (mode == 0)
                mode = burst;
        else
                mode = (mode == 1) ? 4 + burst : 6;

        r.h.al = mode;
        r.h.ah = 0;     /* "Set mode" function call(0) */

        int86(0x10, inregs, outregs);   /* Set new mode */

}
```

This function uses the Lattice intdos() function, which allows MS-DOS function calls to be made. The header file dos.h contains definitions and structures that are used by this function.

Example

```
BASIC                    10 SCREEN(1,0)


C                        main()
                         {

                                 screen(1, 0);

                         }
```

SGN

BASIC Format:	SGN(X)
C Format:	sgn(x)
	x may be any numeric type
Return Type:	int

The SGN, or signum, function returns an integer value to indicate whether its argument is positive, negative, or equal to 0.

Although a signum function is not part of the C function set, one can be easily constructed. Since SGN in BASIC can accept any numeric type, this is an ideal operation to program through a macro definition. In BASIC, SGN returns $+1$ if its argument is positive, -1 if the argument is negative, and 0 when the argument is equal to 0. The macro definition follows:

```
#define sgn((X))   ((X) == 0) ? 0 : (X) / abs((X))
```

This macro simply returns a 0 when the argument is equal to 0 and the argument divided by the absolute value of the argument when it is equal to anything else. This means that if the argument is negative, a −1 will always be returned. If it is positive, then the return value will always be +1.

Example

BASIC   10 PRINT SGN(-14)

C   #define sgn((X)   ((X) == 0) ? ....etc.
                               main()
                               {

                                   printf("%d\n", sgn(-14));

                               }

SHELL

BASIC Format: SHELL "command"
C Format: system("command")
Return Type: int

The SHELL statement in BASIC temporarily transfers control to the operating system, allowing DOS commands to be executed when in BASIC. For instance:

SHELL"DIR"

causes BASIC to reenter DOS and list the directory by means of the DIR command. Once execution of this command is terminated, control returns to BASIC.

In C you may translate SHELL directly to system(). This C function allows the operating system to be accessed from the C program. All DOS commands may serve as arguments to system(). They take the form of quoted strings or assigned char array variables.

Example

BASIC   10 SHELL"DIR"

C   main()
                               {

                                   system("DIR");

                               }
```
```

SIN

BASIC Format:	SIN(X#)
C Format:	sin(x)
	double sin(), x
Return Type:	double

The SIN function returns the trigonometric sine of an argument, which should be expressed as a floating point value.

The UNIX math set contains the sin() function, which is used as a direct replacement for SIN in BASIC. Like other UNIX math functions, sin() expects a double-precision argument and returns a double-precision value. For that reason, sin() must be declared double in any program or function that calls it.

Example

BASIC

```
10 X#=23.154
20 PRINT SIN(X#)
```

C

```
main()
{

    double x, sin();

    x = 23.154;

    printf("%lf\n", sin(x));

}
```

SQR

BASIC Format:	SQR(X#)
C Format:	sqrt(x)
	double x
Return Type:	double

The SQR function returns the square root of its argument. The UNIX math function set contains a direct equivalent of SQR, called sqrt(). As is the case with most complex math functions, this one must be declared double by any program that calls it. It accepts only double arguments and returns doubles as well.

Example

BASIC   10 PRINT SQR(10)

C   main()
                             {

                                 double sqrt();

                                 printf("%lf\n", sqrt((double 10)));

STR$

BASIC Format:	A$ = STR$(X)
C Format:	str$(a$, (double) x)
	char a$[80]
	x is any numeric type
Return Type:	None

The STR$ function returns the value in its numeric argument as a string. The argument may be any numeric data type.

There is no standard function in C that can be used to emulate STR$, so it is necessary to write a special function to accomplish this same operation. The function discussed here is called str$() and requires two arguments. The first is the char array, which will be assigned the string equivalent of the numeric argument. The second is the numeric argument, which is coerced to a double by the (double) cast operator. This function requires a double-precision second argument, and the cast operator makes certain that it gets one.

Within the function, sprintf() writes the double argument to a char array. First, however, the numeric argument is checked for any fractional component. If none exists, the value is written to the array as an integer. Otherwise, it is written as a double, with the decimal point and fractional portion intact.

```
str$(a, b)      /* Assign numeric value in b to a as a string */
char *a;
double b;
{

    if ((b - (int) b) == 0)
        sprintf(a, " %d", (int) b);   /* Assign integer value */
    else
        sprintf(a, " %lf", b);    /* Assign float value */

}
```

This function will write an integer value to the string array when there is no fractional value other than 0; otherwise, it writes a double-precision value to the array. This argument must have a double numeric argument to work properly. Therefore, integer values would be converted to doubles by means of the (double) cast operator or by direct conversion by tacking on a .0 as a fractional component.

Example

BASIC

```
10 A$=STR$(1234)
20 PRINT A$
```

C

```
main()
{

    char a[20];

    str$(a, (double) 1234);

    printf("%s\n", a);

}
```

Note: Stay away from making conversions that must return a string value. This is certainly possible in C, but it can lead to some complex misunderstandings among beginners to this language. A function that returns a string actually returns a pointer to that string. In situations when you want to print the returns of two calls to the same function, unexpected results can occur.

SWAP

BASIC Format:	SWAP A$,B$, SWAP A,B
C Format:	swap$(a$, b$, swap(a, b, swapvar)
	char a$[80], b$[80]
	a and b may be any numeric type
Return Type:	None

The SWAP statement exchanges the values of two variables. Variables in BASIC may be of any type. SWAP may be translated in two different ways, depending on whether numeric values or string values are being exchanged. When the variables are strings, the swap$() function is used. When they are numeric types, swap() is used. The latter is a *macro*, not a function.

The macro is as follows:

```
#define swap((A), (B), (C))    (C)=(A);(A)=(B);(B)=(C)
```

In this usage, it is necessary to provide swap() with a third variable, which is necessary for temporary storage of (A) during the swapping process.

Example

BASIC

```
10 X%=15
20 Y%=20
30 SWAP X%,Y%
```

C

```
#define swap((A), (B)....etc.
main()
{

        int a, b, temp;

        a = 15;
        b = 20;

        swap(a, b, temp);

}
```

When either of these programs has finished executing, the end result is a swapping of the values of the two variables. In the C program example, a third variable of the same type as the other two is also declared. This variable is used for temporary storage of one of the values to be exchanged.

When two string variables are to be swapped, the swap$() function is used. Although the macro could be used to swap pointers, this would eventually lead to serious problems, since pointers cannot be treated in exactly the same manner as variables in C. The following function will swap the values of two strings in C:

```
swap$(a, b)
char a[], b[];
{

        char temp[256];  /* Make temp very large */

        strcpy(temp, a); /* Copy string in a to temp */
        strcpy(a, b);    /* Copy string in b to a */
        strcpy(b, temp); /* Copy string in temp to b */

}
```

This could also be written as a macro, as follows:

```
#define swap$(A, B, C)   strcpy(C, A); strcpy(A, B); strcpy(B, C)
```

However, it is usually better to go with functions rather than macros whenever it is feasible or convenient to do so. The following example uses the swap$() function.

Example

```
BASIC              10 A$="HELLO"
                   20 B$="-GOODBYE"
                   30 SWAP A$,B$
C                  main()
                   {

                        char a[20], b[20];

                        strcpy(a, "HELLO");
                        strcpy(b, "-GOODBYE");

                        swap$(a, b);

                   }
```

TAN

BASIC Format:	TAN(X#)
C Format:	tan(x)
	double tan(), x
Return Type:	double

The TAN function returns the tangent of its argument, which is expressed as an angle in radians.

You can make a direct substitution of the UNIX math function called tan() in performing this translation. This function must be declared double by any program that calls it. Arguments to tan() must also be doubles. Providing another data type to the function can cause the return value to be incorrect. Therefore, make certain that tan() is always used with an argument that is a double-precision type.

Example

```
BASIC              10 X#=14.359
                   20 PRINT TAN(X#)
```

(*continued*)

```
                         main()
                         {

                             double x, tan();

                             x = 14.359;

                             printf("%lf\n", tan(x));

                         }
```

TIME$

BASIC Format:	TIME or TIME$ = string
C Format:	time$() or settime(string)
	char *time$(), *string
Return Type:	char *

In BASIC, TIME$ is a multipurpose variable or statement that sets or returns the system time. When used with a trailing equals sign (=), it is a statement that sets the time to the same values indicated by the string format.

The time is always set or returned in the following format:

hours:minutes:seconds:hundredth.seconds

This is a machine-dependent operation, so no standard function is available to accomplish the retrieval or setting of the time by accessing the computer's internal clock. It is fairly simple to access the various DOS functions that are used to set or retrieve the system time. However, this information must be deciphered and broken down considerably to arrive at the format of display offered by BASIC. Also, since TIME$ may be used as a statement or a variable, two C functions must be written— one to set time, the other to read time. In the following examples, time$() is used to read time and settime() is used to set the system clock. The time$() function to read system time is as follows:

```
char *time$()   /* Return system time as a string */
{

    char a[20], hours[5], minutes[5], seconds[5], hunds[5];
    union REGS r, *inregs, *outregs;

    inregs = &r;
    outregs = &r;

    r.h.ah = 0x2c;    /* "Get time" function call (2ch) */

    intdos(inregs, inregs);   /* Get time */
```

```
/* The following routine puts a string representation of the
various time elements in string a. Leading zeros(0) are inserted
when any value is less than 10 as per BASIC format custom */

      /* hour value in ch register */
      sprintf(hours, "%s%d:", (r.h.ch < 10) ? "0" : "", r.h.ch);
      /* minute value in cl register */
      sprintf(minutes, "%s%d:", (r.h.cl < 10) ? "0" : "", r.h.cl);
      /* seconds value in dh register */
      sprintf(seconds, "%s%d.", (r.h.dh < 10) ? "0" : "", r.h.dh);
      /* seconds/100 in dl register */
      sprintf(hunds, "%s%d", (r.h.dl < 10) ? "0" : "", r.h.dl);

      sprintf(a, "%s%s%s%s", hours, minutes, seconds, hunds);

      return(a);      /* Return time as a string */

}
```

Note that time$() is declared char * at the beginning of the function or program that calls it, as it will return the time as a string and in the standard C format described above.

Example

```
BASIC                    10 PRINT TIME$


C                        main()
                         {

                            char *time$();

                            printf("%s\n", time$());

                         }
```

When system time is set, settime() is used with the same argument that would be passed to TIME$ in a BASIC program:

```
settime(a)      /* Set system time */
char *a;
{

      int h, m, s, hun, l, x;
      char temp[20];
      union REGS r, *inregs, *outregs;

      strcpy(temp, a);  /* Copy string to a temporary variable */
```

(continued)

```
1 = strlen(temp);      /* 1 = length of argument string */
x = 0;
inregs = &r;
outregs = &r;

h = atoi(temp);   /* h = hours (VAL of temp) */
```

/* The following routine extracts the minutes, seconds and
seconds/100 values from the argument string. As in BASIC, it is
not necessary to include all of these elements. Any portion of the
time string that is not included is set to zero */

```
while (temp[x] != ':' && x < 1)
    temp[x++] = ' ';   /* Move to next numeric sequence */

temp[x] = ' ';
m = atoi(temp);    /* m = minute value of string */

while (temp[x] != ':' && x < 1)
    temp[x++] = ' ';   /* Move to next numeric sequence */

temp[x] = ' ';
s = atoi(temp);    /* s = seconds portion of string */

while (temp[x] != '.' && x < 1)
    temp[x++] = ' ';   /* Move to next numeric sequence */

temp[x] = ' ';
hun = atoi(temp);    /* hun = seconds/100 portion of string */
```

/* The following lines assign the extracted numeric values from
the argument string to their appropriate registers */

```
r.h.ch = h;
r.h.cl = m;
r.h.dh = s;
r.h.dl = hun;
r.h.ah = 0x2d;      /* "Set time" function call (2dh) */
intdos(inregs, outregs);      /* Set time */
}
```

This function and the one before it seem to be quite complex; however, the complexities involve formatting the time information, not the actual retrieval or setting process.

Example

```
BASIC                      10 TIME$="14:34:48.34"


C                          main()
                           {

                               settime("14:34:48.34")

                           }
```

The settime() function is written so that it is not necessary to include every element of the complete time format (that is, hours, minutes, seconds, hundredths of seconds). You may include only hours; hours and minutes; hours, minutes, and seconds, and so forth. This function will use whatever argument you provide and set the clock accordingly. For instance, if you simply supplied settime() with an argument of "14", the clock would be set to 14:00:00.00.

VAL

BASIC Format:	VAL(A$)
C Format:	atof(a$)
	double atof()
	char *a$
Return Type:	double

The VAL function returns any numeric value found in its string argument. VAL skips over leading whitespaces and converts numeric characters to their equivalent numeric values.

There are several C functions that can be used to replace VAL, but atof() probably comes closest to emulating it in most ways. This function returns the numeric value found in a string argument as a double-precision number. Variations of atof() include atoi(), which returns the numeric value in a string as an integer.

Example

```
BASIC                    10 A$="123.513"
                         20 X#=VAL(A$)


C                        main()
                         {

                             char *a;
                             double x, atof();

                             a = "123.513";
                             x = atof(a);

                         }
```

WHILE/WEND

BASIC Format:	WHILE expression
	(loop statements)
	WEND

C Format: while (expression)
                            loop statement(s);
Return Type: None

The WHILE/WEND statements in BASIC form a loop that executes a series of statements as long as the expression is true.
      A direct translation of WHILE/WEND is made using the while statement in C.
This is used to form a while loop.

Example

BASIC

```
10 X%=100
20 WHILE X%>0
30 PRINT X%
40 X%=X%-1
50 WEND
```

C

```
main()
{

    int x;

    x = 100;
    while (x > 0) {
            printf("%d\n", x);
            --x;
    }

}
```

WIDTH

BASIC Format: WIDTH size
C Format: width(size)
                            int size
Return Type: None

The WIDTH statement in BASIC sets the output line width of the screen, printer, or
other device in terms of character number.
      This statement addresses several different devices but is best known for its
control of the color screen. The following function emulates the action of WIDTH
when it is used to set the screen to 40 or 80 character mode:

```
width(x)     /* Set width of screen to 40 or 80 columns */
int x;
{

     int mode;
     union REGS r, *inregs, *outregs;

     inregs = &r;
     outregs = &r;
     r.h.ah = 15;     /* "Determine current mode" video call (15) */

     int86(0x10, inregs, outregs);    /* Get current mode */

     if (r.h.al == 7 || r.h.ah == x)
          return;    /* If using monochrome card - do nothing */
     else if (x == 80)
          mode = r.h.al + 2;    /* Set color mode 80 */
     else if (x == 40)
          mode = r.h.al - 2;    /* Set color mode 40 */

     r.h.ah = 0;        /* "Set mode" video call (0) */
     r.h.al = mode;     /* new mode value */

     int86(0x10, inregs, outregs); /* Set new mode */

}
```

This function uses the int86() function common to Lattice C and several other C compilers and interpreters to perform an 8086 interrupt at several places in its execution chain. The width() function must determine the current video mode and make changes in the mode accordingly. For instance, if the screen is in medium-resolution color mode, a call to width(80) will cause it to go into high-resolution video mode (SCREEN 2).

Index